Questi
Bible Study Guide

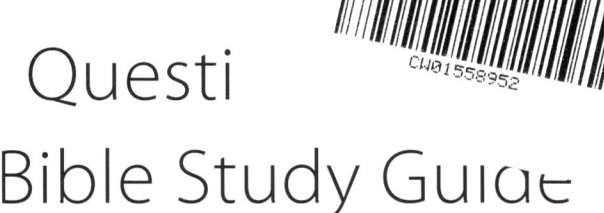

Worry Less;
Live More

Good Questions
Have Groups Talking

By Josh Hunt

Contents

Worry Less; Live More, Lesson #1
The Practice of Rejoicing
Good Questions Have Groups Talking
www.joshhunt.com

OPEN:

What is one thing that is on your mind these days?

DIG

1. Don't worry, be happy. Is this message of that song biblical?

Remember that eighties song "Don't Worry, Be Happy"? (You're singing along right now, aren't you?) Well, it's not only a fun song with a great reggae beat, but it's also good advice. "Don't worry, be happy" is a good motto to adopt, because worry will steal your joy faster than you can say "leg warmers."

Worry is a sneaky thing. You might start the day just thinking about a situation in your life, but if you think too long, you will end up in full-out worry mode. You will start thinking things like, If those layoffs really happen at our company, I don't know what we'll do. We just barely make it now. What if I can't get another job with health insurance? What if I don't get a severance package? What if? What if? What if?

Don't let your thoughts take you there. If you cross over into the land of worry, you will eventually drive into the territory of fear and ultimately hit the city limits of despair. It's not worth it! Besides, no matter how much you worry, it doesn't change the situation one single bit, right? Prayer is what changes things.

Worry is not only a happiness stealer, it's a sin. The Bible instructs us not to worry. Matthew 6:34 says, "Therefore do not worry about tomorrow, for tomorrow will worry about itself. Each day has enough trouble of its own" (NIV).

That's pretty clear, isn't it?

Worry is a hard habit to break, especially if you have lived your whole life as a worrywart. But it's not impossible to overcome. How do I know? I was a world-class worrier for many years. I'd think about something for a while and eventually work myself into such a tizzy that I wanted to hide under the covers and eat bonbons all day. Ever been there?

If you have been taking regular trips to the land of worry, get off that highway. Take the prayer detour and stay on that road until you reach your final destination of peace, happiness, and victory. And while you're "in the car," pop in an eighties CD and sing along with "Don't Worry, Be Happy." Good tunes always make the journey more fun! (MMA) — Michelle Medlock Adams, Ramona Richards, and Katherine Anne Douglas, *Wonderfully Made: Devotional Thoughts on Becoming a Beautiful Woman of God* (Uhrichsville, OH: Barbour Publishing, Inc., 2012).

2. Philippians 3.1, 4.4. Rejoice always. Sounds kind of light and fluffy. Why is it important—and it seems quite important—that we get happy?

IF YOU WERE TO ASK a roomful of people what God wants us to do, you'd likely get a wide range of answers.

Some people would say he wants us to obey him or to be holy. Others might claim he wants us to love people and stand up for peace and justice. But chances are, you wouldn't hear anyone say, "God wants us to be happy."

Most of us have a complicated relationship with happiness. We all want to be happy, but we may feel guilty about this longing. Isn't it selfish to pursue happiness? Isn't it more spiritual to frown than to smile?

In a world full of brokenness, we may wonder if happiness is a worthy pursuit. If we are seeking to follow Jesus, should this quest be written off as superficial and unspiritual?

Maybe you've been taught over the years that God cares about your holiness, not your happiness. This implies we have to choose between the two.

We've also heard that God calls us to joy, not happiness. According to innumerable sermons and books and blog posts, there's a big difference between joy, which is spiritual, and happiness, which is unspiritual. But does the Bible actually say this? Does God care about our happiness?

The answer might surprise you. Yes, God does care about our happiness. And he has gone to great lengths to prove it. — Randy Alcorn, *Does God Want Us to Be Happy? The Case for Biblical Happiness* (Carol Stream, IL: Tyndale House Publishers, Inc., 2019).

3. I have heard people say that God cares about our joy, but not about our happiness. Is that right?

Among Christ-followers, happiness was once a positive, desirable word.

Scottish churchman Thomas Boston (1676–1732) said, "Consider what man is. He is a creature that desires happiness, and cannot but desire it. The desire of happiness is woven into his nature, and cannot be eradicated. It is as natural for him to desire it as it is to breathe."[3]

Evangelist George Whitefield (1714–1770) said, "Is it the end of religion to make men happy, and is it not every one's privilege to be as happy as he can?"[4]

Whitefield once asked an audience, "Does [Jesus] want your heart only for the same end as the devil does, to make you miserable? No, he only wants you to believe on him, that you might be saved. This, this, is all the dear Savior desires, to make you happy, that you may leave your sins, to sit down eternally with him."[5]

Pastor Charles Spurgeon (1834–1892) said to his London congregation almost 150 years ago, "My dear Brothers and Sisters, if anybody in the world ought to be happy, we are the people. . . . How boundless our privileges! How brilliant our hopes!"[6]

Boston, Whitefield, and Spurgeon are just three Christian leaders among many throughout church history who knew that happiness is one of God's greatest gifts.

Let's be clear: we all know that happiness at the expense of others is wrong.

Is there selfish and superficial happiness? Sure. There's also selfish and superficial love, peace, loyalty, and trust. But we don't villainize these virtues just because they are sometimes misguided. Likewise, we shouldn't throw out Christ-centered and God-honoring happiness with the bathwater of self-centered happiness. — Randy Alcorn, *Does God Want Us to Be Happy? The Case for Biblical Happiness* (Carol Stream, IL: Tyndale House Publishers, Inc., 2019).

4. T/F God is more interested in our holiness than our happiness.

Some Christians see happiness as the virtual opposite of holiness. But Scripture says otherwise.

Consider Leviticus 9:24: "Fire came out from the presence of the LORD and consumed the burnt offering . . . on the altar. And when all the people saw it, they shouted for joy and fell facedown" (NIV).

The radically holy God sent down fire, and the people did what? They fell facedown . . . and "shouted for joy"! This remarkable response flows from the utter holiness of submission combined with the utter happiness of praise.

To be holy is to see God as he is and to become like him, covered in Christ's righteousness. And since God's nature is to be happy (as we saw in chapter 2), the more like him we become in our sanctification, the happier we will be.

We see this link between happiness and holiness in many passages, including this one: "Let your priests be clothed with righteousness, and let your saints shout for joy" (Psalm 132:9).

Greek scholar J. B. Phillips (1906–1982) translated Revelation 20:6 this way: "Happy and holy is the one who shares in the first resurrection!" Similarly, the most literal English version, Young's Literal Translation, renders it "Happy and holy [is] he who is having part in the first rising again."

Most translations of this verse read "blessed and holy," with the result that modern readers (unaware that in old English blessed meant happy) understand the sentence as containing two adjectives of consecration. But when the Greek is rendered "happy and holy," readers can realize, Wow, so those who know God are not only holy but also happy? Happiness is what I've been searching for! Maybe I should stop dividing my life into "church me," in which I try to be holy, and "world me," in which I seek to be happy.

Any understanding of God is utterly false if it is incompatible with the lofty and infinitely holy view of God in Ezekiel 1:26-28 and Isaiah 6:1-4 and of Jesus in Revelation 1:9-18. God is decidedly and unapologetically anti-sin, but he is in no sense anti-happiness. Indeed, holiness is exactly what secures our happiness. Spurgeon said, "Holiness is the royal road to happiness. The death of sin is the life of joy."[7]

Holiness doesn't mean abstaining from pleasure; holiness means recognizing Jesus as the source of life's greatest pleasure. — Randy Alcorn, *Does God Want Us to Be Happy? The Case for Biblical Happiness* (Carol Stream, IL: Tyndale House Publishers, Inc., 2019).

5. How does the unhappy Christian harm the cause of Christ?

If we want to be happy but God doesn't want us to be happy, wouldn't that be bad news?

The gospel is called the "good news of happiness" (Isaiah 52:7, ESV, NASB). Then why do Christians today often say things like "God wants you blessed, not happy"[7] and "God doesn't want you to be happy. God wants you to be holy"?[8]

Any message that God doesn't want us to be happy undermines the "good news of happiness" Jesus came to bring us. Compelling biblical evidence and a long history of Christ-followers have affirmed that our God is pro-happiness.

What if a happy God made us for happiness, and therefore our desire to be happy is inseparable from our longing for God?

What if God wired his image bearers for happiness before sin entered the world?

What if wanting happiness isn't the problem, but looking for happiness in sin is?

What if our desire to be happy can be properly redirected to God and all that he wants for us?

How might this perspective on happiness change our approach to life, parenting, church, ministry, business, sports, entertainment, and everything else?

Since unhappy Christians make the gospel unattractive, wouldn't the gospel become contagiously appealing if Christians embraced happiness in Jesus? — Randy Alcorn, *Does God Want Us to Be Happy? The Case for Biblical Happiness* (Carol Stream, IL: Tyndale House Publishers, Inc., 2019).

6. Galatians 4.6. What does "Abba" mean? What does this teach us about God?

Abba was an ordinary family word of Jesus' day. It conveyed intimacy, tenderness, dependence, and complete lack of fear or anxiety. Modern English equivalents would be Daddy or Papa.

No Jew would have dreamed of using this very intimate term to address God. However, Jesus always used this word in His prayers (Aramaic abba or its Greek equivalent pater), with the exception of His cry from the cross. — David Jeremiah, *David Jeremiah Morning and Evening Devotions: Holy Moments in the Presence of God* (Nashville: Thomas Nelson, 2017).

7. What does this teach us about happiness?

How many of us have ever heard a sermon, read a book, had a discussion about, or meditated on God's happiness? In fact, we're often taught to do exactly the opposite—to squelch our longing for happiness (which will never work).

The resulting silence about or contradiction of biblical revelation about one of God's great attributes is an immense loss to individuals and families, as well as to the church as a whole.

The title of this book is ironic. If we were thinking correctly, we would naturally wonder, Why would anyone even ask whether God wants his people to be happy?

Some unbelievers might be perplexed by the question "Does God want us to be happy?" If they did believe in a good God, surely they'd suppose he would value his children's happiness. What good father wouldn't?

Have you ever met a loving, devoted human father who doesn't want his children to be happy? Sure, he wouldn't want them to sacrifice personal integrity or virtue. But he knows that not having those things will never make them happy anyway! He wants them to make good and right choices that result in their long-term happiness.

The question "Does God want us to be happy?" makes sense to many of us only because we have been indoctrinated to believe he doesn't. That's what I was taught after becoming a Christian as a teenager. Millions of others have been taught the same.

I'm delighted to say that the Bible itself, along with the beliefs of people throughout church history, have liberated me from this misconception. — Randy Alcorn, *Does God Want Us to Be Happy? The Case for Biblical Happiness* (Carol Stream, IL: Tyndale House Publishers, Inc., 2019).

8. Psalm 42.5. (Look also at the context.) Can we just decide not to be downcast? Can we just choose to be happy?

Happiness is basically a choice which is not dependent upon situations or conditions. Each of us is responsible for our own happiness. Happiness can be enhanced by what occurs around us or what our spouse does, but we are more likely to be happy if we center our activities on others instead of on ourselves.

Dr. Archibald Hart suggests writing the following affirmations on cards, keeping them with you, and reading them periodically.

Just for today I will set my affection on things above, not on things on the earth.

Just for today I will not worry about what will happen tomorrow, but will trust that God will go before me into the unknown.

Just for today I will endure anything that hurts or depresses me because I believe God controls what happens to me.

Just for today I will not dwell on my misfortunes. I will replace my negative thoughts with happy and hopeful thoughts.

Just for today I will choose to do some things I do not like doing, and I will do them cheerfully and with a happy spirit.

Just for today I will make a conscious effort to love those who don't show love to me and be kind to those who do not appreciate me.

Just for today I will be patient with those who irritate me and longsuffering toward those who are selfish and inconsiderate.

Just for today I will forgive all those who hurt me— even forgiving myself.

Just for today I will choose to BE HAPPY! — H. Norman Wright, *Quiet Times for Couples* (Eugene, OR: Harvest House, 2011).

9. **Psalm 19:8, Romans 8:28, Philippians 4:19, Philippians 1:21, Romans 12:1–2, 1 Thessalonians 5:16–18. What reasons do you find for rejoicing in these passages?**

We rejoice in His precepts and promises.

We can rejoice in His providence.

We can rejoice in His pardon.

We can rejoice in His paths and purposes for us.

We can rejoice in His provision, for our God will supply all our needs.

We can rejoice in His protection, for He will never leave us or forsake us.

We can rejoice in His paradise, for to live is Christ and to die is gain (Philippians 1:21).

Robert J. Morgan, *Worry Less, Live More: God's Prescription for a Better Life* (Nashville: Thomas Nelson, 2017).

10. Rejoicing is a command that God has given. It is a choice we make. How? How do we make the choice to rejoice?

But if I ever find myself in a bad mood, I immediately make a choice to be happy. In fact, it is the first choice I make every day. I say out loud to my mirror, 'Today, I will choose to be happy!' I smile into the mirror and laugh even if I am sad. I just say, 'Ha, ha, ha, ha!' And soon, I am happy, exactly as I have chosen to be."

David was now shaking his head in wonder. "You are a very special young lady, Miss Frank."

"Thank you," Anne [Frank] said. "That is also a choice."

David leaned forward. "Really," he said with his eyebrows raised. "You've got me now. Explain."

"My life—my personality, my habits, even my speech—is a combination of the books I choose to read, the people I choose to listen to, and the thoughts I choose to tolerate in my mind. Before the war, when I was a little girl, my papa took me to Het Vondel Park on a Saturday afternoon to hear the orchestra play. At the end of the concert, from behind the musicians, a hundred helium balloons of red and blue and yellow and green floated up into the sky. It was so exciting!

"I tugged on Papa's arm and asked, 'Papa, which color balloon will go the highest?' And he said to me, 'Anne, it's not the color of the balloon that is important. It's what's inside that makes all the difference.' "

For a moment, Anne was quiet and the attic still. She seemed so deep in thought that David barely breathed. Then she looked David directly in the eye, lifted her chin, and said, "Mr. Ponder, I don't believe that being Jewish or Aryan or African has any bearing on what one can become. Greatness does not care if one is a girl or a boy. If, in fact, it is what's inside us that makes all the difference, then the difference is made when we choose what goes inside." — Andy Andrews, *The Traveler's Gift: Seven Decisions That Determine Personal Success* (Nashville: Thomas Nelson, 2005).

11. Who has been an example to you of someone who made the choice to rejoice?

My mother has always been a happy person. It didn't matter if it was raining outside. It didn't matter if our air-conditioning went out in mid-July. It didn't matter if one of her friends talked ugly to her. Mom has always chosen happiness. Growing up, Mom's happiness bugged me. She'd begin each day something like this. She'd burst into my bedroom, flip on my light switch, and begin her very loud rendition of "This is the day that the Lord has made. Let us rejoice and be glad in it." She'd sing at the top of her lungs and occasionally clap in time, as well. What a way to start the day, eh? There was no sleeping in at our house, because if you didn't get up, she'd just start another verse!

After my father passed away last year, I didn't hear my mom singing anymore. I worried about her. I prayed to God, "Please restore the song back into my mother's life." After a period of grieving, little by little, I saw Mom's happiness return. It started with a hum, and now she's all-out singing again. I'm still waiting for that loud clapping to return, but I'm sure it's in the works. Why? Because Mom doesn't base her happiness on her circumstances. Sure, she's lonely without Daddy, but she chooses to be happy because of Jesus. She chooses to focus on the beauty in life—not the tragedy.

How is your happiness level? If it has been a while since you've burst forth in song, give it a whirl! Sing praises unto God until you sing yourself happy. But you say, "Michelle, you don't know what I'm going through right now. There's no way I can be happy." You may be right. But through Jesus you can be happy. Job 8:21 says, "He will yet fill your mouth with laughter and your lips with shouts of joy" (NIV). That's a promise you can count on! He will—but you have to want it.

You have to choose happiness. Comic writer Robert Orben once said, "Happiness is contagious. Be a carrier!" That's pretty good advice. If you choose to be happy, you'll discover more people will want to be around you. Being happy simply makes you more attractive. Your happiness will be infectious. Happiness will become a lifelong habit, as it has been for my mom. You may even find yourself humming happily all day long. Beware: Loud clapping is soon to follow! Go ahead—choose happiness today! It's a beautiful life! (MMA) — Michelle Medlock Adams, Ramona Richards, and Katherine Anne Douglas, *Wonderfully Made: Devotional Thoughts on*

Becoming a Beautiful Woman of God (Uhrichsville, OH: Barbour Publishing, Inc., 2012).

12. Imagine two people. One chooses happiness; the other does not. Other than their happiness, how else are their lives different?

Beginning this very moment, I am a happy person, for I now truly understand the concept of happiness. Few others before me have been able to grasp the truth of the physical law that enables one to live happily every day. I know now that happiness is not an emotional phantom floating in and out of my life. Happiness is a choice. Happiness is the end result of certain thoughts and activities, which actually bring about a chemical reaction in my body. This reaction results in a euphoria that, while elusive to some, is totally under my control.

Today I will choose to be happy. I will greet each day with laughter.

Within moments of awakening, I will laugh for seven seconds. Even after such a small period of time, excitement has begun to flow through my bloodstream. I feel different. I am different! I am enthusiastic about the day. I am alert to its possibilities. I am happy!

Laughter is an outward expression of enthusiasm, and I know that enthusiasm is the fuel that moves the world. I laugh throughout the day. I laugh while I am alone, and I laugh in conversation with others. People are drawn to me because I have laughter in my heart. The world belongs to the enthusiastic, for people will follow them anywhere!

Today I will choose to be happy. I will smile at every person I meet.

My smile has become my calling card. It is, after all, the most potent weapon I possess. My smile has the strength to forge bonds, break ice, and calm storms. I will use my smile constantly. Because of my smile, the people with whom I come in contact on a daily basis will choose to further my causes and follow my leadership. I will always smile first. That particular display of a good attitude will tell others what I expect in return.

My smile is the key to my emotional makeup. A wise man once said, "I do not sing because I am happy; I am happy because I sing!" When I choose to smile, I become the master of my emotions. Discouragement, despair, frustration, and fear will always wither when confronted by my smile. The power of who I am is displayed when I smile.

Today I will choose to be happy. I am the possessor of a grateful spirit.

In the past, I have found discouragement in particular situations until I compared the condition of my life to others less fortunate. Just as a fresh breeze cleans smoke from the air, so a grateful spirit removes the cloud of despair. It is impossible for the seeds of depression to take root in a thankful heart.

My God has bestowed upon me many gifts, and for these I will remember to be grateful. Too many times I have offered up the prayers of a beggar, always asking for more and forgetting to give thanks. I do not wish to be seen as a greedy child, unappreciative and disrespectful. I am grateful for sight and sound and breath. If ever in my life there is a pouring out of blessings beyond that, then I will be grateful for the miracle of abundance.

I will greet each day with laughter. I will smile at every person I meet. I am the possessor of a grateful spirit.

Today I will choose to be happy. — Andy Andrews, *The Traveler's Gift: Seven Decisions That Determine Personal Success* (Nashville: Thomas Nelson, 2005).

13. Philippians is considered the letter of joy. We already looked at two verses from this book. Let's look at a few more. Philippians 1.3 – 6. What do we learn about how to rejoice in the Lord always from this passage?

The apostle Paul's joy was unrelated to his circumstances. If it had been tied to pleasures on earth, possessions, freedom, prestige, outward success, or a good reputation, he wouldn't have had any joy.

Paul's joy was centered on his ministry and was indifferent toward all other things. That's why he could tell the Philippians, "I thank my God upon every remembrance of you, always in every prayer of mine making request for you with all joy" (Phil. 1:3–4). He had joy in spite of trouble, as long as Christ's cause was advanced. He had joy in spite of detractors, as long as Christ's name was proclaimed. He had joy in spite of death, as long as Christ was exalted. And he had joy in spite of the flesh, as long as Christ's church was assisted. — John MacArthur, *Truth for Today: A Daily Touch of God's Grace* (Nashville, Tenn.: J. Countryman, 2001), 363.

14. What was Paul's situation as he wrote this? Was he vacationing at Disneyland?

Though Paul was under house arrest in Rome when he wrote to the Philippians, his mind wasn't bound. Often he reflected on his experiences with the Philippian

Christians. As he did so, his thoughts turned to prayers of praise and thanksgiving for all the Lord had done through them.

I'm sure Paul remembered when he preached in Philippi and God opened Lydia's heart to believe the gospel (Acts 16:13–14). Subsequently everyone in her household was saved (v. 15). Surely her kindness and hospitality were bright spots in an otherwise stormy stay at Philippi.

He must also have remembered the demon-possessed girl whom the Lord delivered from spiritual bondage (v. 18), and the Philippian jailer who threw Paul and Silas into prison after they had been beaten severely (vv. 23–24). Perhaps the girl became part of the Philippian church—the text doesn't say. We do know that the jailer and his whole household were saved, after which they showed kindness to Paul and Silas by tending to their wounds and feeding them (vv. 30–34).

The many financial gifts the Philippians sent to Paul were also fond memories for him because they were given out of love and concern. That was true of their present gift as well, which was delivered by Epaphroditus and went far beyond Paul's need (Phil. 4:18).

Paul's gratitude illustrates that Christian joy is enhanced in your life by your ability to recall the goodness of others. A corollary is your ability to forgive shortcomings and unkindnesses. That goes against the grain of our "don't get mad—get even" society, but is perfectly consistent with the compassion and forgiveness God has shown you. Therefore, be quick to forgive evil and slow to forget good. — John F. MacArthur Jr., *Drawing Near—Daily Readings for a Deeper Faith* (Wheaton, IL: Crossway Books, 1993), 53.

15. Philippians 1.18 – 25. Read over this passage silently. Look for every time Paul uses the word "rejoice." What do we learn about rejoicing in the Lord always from this passage?

A few years ago my radio ministry heard from a listener who was exhibiting exactly the right attitude in the face of a terminal illness. A teenager from the Midwest sent a prayer request concerning her recently diagnosed Lou Gehrig's disease. That Christian young woman, who by now is probably with the Lord, accepted her condition with grace and optimism. Here is part of what she wrote to us: "I love the Lord very much and feel the Lord is using my condition to work in different peoples' lives. Please pray with me that He would continue to use me no matter what the outcome."

Her sentiments were right in step with Philippians 1:21, in which the apostle Paul proclaims his joy and confidence at the possibility of death. What enabled him to rejoice was his complete confidence in the Word of God.

Earlier Paul had articulated his trust in God's promises when he wrote these familiar words in Romans 8:28, "We know that God causes all things to work together for good to those who love God, to those who are called according to His purpose." Now he shared verbatim with the Philippians from Job 13:16, "For I know that this shall turn out for my deliverance" (Phil. 1:19). That too was a trustworthy promise from the Word, and it made Paul confident that his current trials would have a positive outcome.

Whether suffering was of long or short duration, Paul knew that the righteous would be delivered from their temporal trials. That was certainly borne out when God restored Job from his difficult, lengthy ordeal of testing.

Knowing all this, and realizing that all of God's written Word is available to us, we can certainly have Paul's type of confidence as we consider the inevitability of death. And we can "keep on rejoicing" (1 Peter 4:13), even if it's the Lord's will that we experience an early departure from this life. — John MacArthur, *Strength for Today* (Wheaton, IL: Crossway Books, 1997).

16. Philippians 2.2. What do we learn about joy from this passage?

Someone has called this letter 'the epistle of joy' and George Duncan wrote a short devotional about it called The Life of Continual Rejoicing.15 Paul introduced us to 'joy' as early as verse 4, and that word, or 'rejoice' or 'rejoicing', occurs thirteen times in this short letter. And always it is in the present tense. His joy is now—even if the main reason is the great and certain hope of future everlasting blessing in Christ. Our joy and rejoicing should always be present tense. If we concentrate only on past joys, we can become wistful and over-nostalgic and get morose. We can get like the man who complained that 'even nostalgia isn't what it used to be!' But if we only anticipate our future joy, failing to rejoice now in our salvation, people will ask where is the 'joy of the Lord' which 'is your strength'16 (my emphasis on 'is'). Even though Jesus told His disciples not to rejoice merely that the spirits were subject to them but that their names were written in heaven,17 He nevertheless urged on them a current joy about their wonderful future certainty. Yes! Rejoice now! Enjoy the journey! — Gerard Chrispin, *Philippians for Today: Priorities from Prison, Exploring the Bible Commentary* (Leominster: Day One, 2005), 120.

17. Philippians 2.17 – 18. What do we learn about joy from this passage?

Paul's joy. The apostle twice sounds the note of joy in verse 17: "Even if I am to be poured out as a drink offering upon the sacrificial offering of your faith, I am glad and rejoice with you all." The sacrificial image Paul evokes was common practice in both pagan and Jewish sacrifices. A priest would offer a sacrifice and then later pour out a sacrificial libation to complement it. So Paul saw the Philippians as priests offering a sacrificial offering of faith, followed by his pouring his own libation over it. Was Paul referring to his death? We do not know. But what is clear is that he viewed his service as a complement or contribution to their service. Paul's Christlike humility flashed bright here because he viewed himself as a complement to their sacrifice and not vice versa.9 At this thought his joy peaked. Literally he said, "I rejoice and co-rejoice with you all."

The Philippians' joy. Paul invites them to join his double-dose of joy with a double-dip of their own: "Likewise you also should be glad and rejoice with me" (v. 18).

The joy note sounds four times in the space of these two verses, and that is very significant. Up to now all mentions of joy (except 1:25) have referenced Paul's joy (cf. 1:4, 18 [twice]; 2:2, 17 [twice]).

But now with this imperative to rejoice, a shift takes place, and their joy will be commanded three times more (cf. 3:1; 4:4). Also, this first imperative was totally meshed with Paul's joy and was a command to rejoice in the midst of suffering.10 What we have here is a partaking of the fellowship of the gospel at its deepest level (cf. 1:5, 7)—a fellowship rooted in the three-way bond of Paul, Christ, and the Philippians.

In fact, the driving theological reality is Christ himself, whose self-humiliation (vv. 6–8) and super-exaltation (vv. 9–11) are the ground of assurance of future victory and the motivating example to "work out your own salvation with fear and trembling, for it is God who works in you, both to will and to work for his good pleasure" (vv. 12, 13). — R. Kent Hughes, *Philippians: The Fellowship of the Gospel, Preaching the Word* (Wheaton, IL: Crossway Books, 2007), 101–102.

18. What if I can't find the grace to rejoice? What to do then?

I am often asked what a Christian should do if the cheerfulness of obedience is not there. It is a good question. My answer is not to simply get on with your duty because feelings are irrelevant! My answer has three steps. First, confess the sin of joylessness. Acknowledge the culpable coldness of your heart. Don't say that it doesn't matter how you feel. Second, pray earnestly that God would restore the joy of obedience. Third, go ahead and do the outward dimension of your duty in the hope that the doing will rekindle the delight. (For more practical counsel on fighting for joy, see appendix 4.)

This is very different from saying, "Do your duty because feelings don't count." These steps are predicated on the assumption that there is such a thing as hypocrisy. They are based on the belief that our goal is the reunion of pleasure and duty and that a justification of their separation is a justification of sin. John Murray puts it like this:

There is no conflict between gratification of desire and the enhancement of man's pleasure, on the one hand, and fulfillment of God's command on the other.... The tension that often exists within us between a sense of duty and wholehearted spontaneity is a tension that arises from sin and a disobedient will. No such tension would have invaded the heart of unfallen man. And the operations of saving grace redirected to the end of removing the tension so that there may be, as there was with man at the beginning, the perfect complementation of duty and pleasure, of commandment and love. — John Piper, *Desiring God* (Sisters, OR: Multnomah Publishers, 2003), 301.

19. What did you learn today? What do you want to remember and apply?

20. How can we pray for each other this week?

Worry Less; Live More, Lesson #2
The Practice of Gentleness
Good Questions Have Groups Talking
www.joshhunt.com

You might challenge your people to memorize Philippians 4.4 – 9 during this study. Nothing will drive steel in your soul like Scripture memory. Lead by example.

OPEN:

What is one thing that you are grateful for today?

DIG

1. Let your gentleness be evident to all. Why is gentleness important?

The first verse I ever memorized would go a long way toward helping us to get along with each other: "Be ye kind one to another." (Ephesians 4:32 KJV) We need to think clearly about the tone of our voices. Science in the Bible agree that the tone of your voice has as much to do with your ability to get along with others as just about anything. The Bible says, "let your gentleness be evident to all." (Philippians 4:5)

For example, take a study where people were given performance feedback – some negative, some positive. If they were given negative performance feedback in a very warm, positive, and upbeat tone, they came out of there feeling pretty good about the interaction. If they were given positive feedback in a very cold, critical, judgmental tone, they came out feeling negative, even about positive feedback. So the emotional subtext is more powerful in many ways than the overt, ostensible interaction that we're having.5

When your mind is transformed through the power of the Holy Spirit using the Word of God to change your mind so that your gentleness is evident to all, your relationships will start to change. You will find it is a whole lot easier to get along with others when your gentleness is evident to all. When you meditate on that truth, your life is changed, and your relationships change. People who were once hard to get along with become much easier to get along with as you meditate on the command to let your gentleness be evident to all. — Josh Hunt, *How to Get Along With Almost Anyone*, 2014.

2. What consequences come to the non-gentle?

If you use a snippy tone, you will get a bad result every single time, even if you are right. — Josh Hunt, *How to Get Along With Almost Anyone*, 2014.

3. Matthew 11.28 – 30. What does Jesus reveal about Himself from this verse?

Jesus described Himself as "'gentle and lowly in heart'" (Matt. 11:29); therefore, He gives rest, not weariness, to all those who submit to Him and do His work. In Christ you have not only a Savior but also a burden bearer. He helps you carry all your burdens, including the burden of obedience.

Jesus will never give you a burden too heavy to carry. His yoke has nothing to do with the demands of the law or human works. Instead, it pertains to the Christian's obedience to Him, which He wants to make a joyful and happy experience. Thank God for providing such a gracious burden bearer in the person of His Son. — John MacArthur, *Truth for Today: A Daily Touch of God's Grace* (Nashville, Tenn.: J. Countryman, 2001), 244.

4. What is a yoke?

The "yoke" Jesus refers to in Matthew 11:29-30 is well illustrated by the process of training a young bullock to plow. In some parts of the world, the farmer will have the young bullock harnessed to the same yoke as a mature ox. The bullock, dwarfed by the other animal, will not even be pulling any of the weight. It is merely learning to walk in a field under control and with a yoke around its neck; the ox pulls all the weight. It is the same when a believer takes Christ's yoke. As the Christian learns, the yoke is easy and the burden light. — Michael P. Green, ed*., Illustrations for Biblical Preaching: Over 1500 Sermon Illustrations Arranged by Topic and Indexed Exhaustively, Revised edition of: The expositor's illustration file.* (Grand Rapids: Baker Book House, 1989).

5. What does it mean that Jesus' yoke is easy?

The answer seems clear. Jesus taught that His yoke is easy. Could it be we have put on some other yoke?

Perhaps we have put on the yoke of religion.

Perhaps we have put on the yoke of duty.

Perhaps we have put on the yoke of feel-good-faith.

Perhaps we have put on the yoke of legalism.

Perhaps we have put on the yoke of moralism.

Perhaps we have put on the yoke of trying really hard to be good.

If the yoke that we have around our neck is not easy, it is not Jesus' yoke.

Ortberg suggests that we have replaced Jesus' yoke with rule-keeping:

> A recent study by the Barna Group found that the number one challenge to helping people grow spiritually is that most people equate spiritual maturity with trying hard to follow the rules in the Bible. No wonder people also said they find themselves unmotivated to pursue spiritual growth. If I think God's aim is to produce rule-followers, spiritual growth will always be an obligation rather than a desire of my heart.
>
> "Rule-keeping does not naturally evolve into living by faith," Paul wrote, "but only perpetuates itself in more and more rule-keeping." In other words, it only results in a rule-keeping, desire-smothering, Bible-reading, emotion-controlling, self-righteous person who is not like me. In the end, I cannot follow God if I don't trust that he really has my best interests at heart.
>
> The letter kills, but the Spirit gives life. There is an enormous difference between following rules and following Jesus, because I can follow rules without cultivating the right heart.

Josh Hunt, *How to Live the Christian Life*, 2016.

6. Weary. What does that feel like? Can you describe a season in life when you were weary?

In August 1930, forty-five-year-old Joseph Crater waved good-bye to friends after an evening meal in a New York restaurant, flagged down a taxi, and rode off. He was never seen or heard from again.

Fifty years of research has offered countless theories but no conclusions. A search of his apartment revealed one clue. It was a note attached to a check, and both were left for his wife. The check was for a sizable amount, and the note simply read, "I am very weary. Love, Joe."

The note could have been nothing more than a thought at the end of a hard day. Or it could have meant a great deal more—the epitaph of a despairing man.

Weariness is tough. I don't mean physical weariness that comes from mowing the lawn or the mental weariness that follows a hard day of decisions and thinking. No, the weariness that attacked Joseph Crater is much worse. It's the weariness that comes just before you give up. That feeling of honest desperation. It's that stage in life when motivation disappears: the children grow up, a job is lost, a spouse dies. The result is weariness—deep, lonely, frustrated weariness.

Only one man in history has claimed to have an answer for it. He stands before all the Joseph Craters of the world with the same promise: "Come to me, all you who are weary . . . and I will give you rest" (Matthew 11:28 NIV). — *On the Anvil* / Max Lucado, *God Is with You Every Day: A 365-Day Devotional* (Nashville: Thomas Nelson, 2015).

7. What is the solution of weariness?

Jesus says he is the solution for weariness of soul.

Go to him. Be honest with him. Admit you have soul secrets you've never dealt with. He already knows what they are. He's just waiting for you to ask him to help....

Go ahead. You'll be glad you did. Those near to you will be glad as well. — Max Lucado, *Everyday Blessings: Inspirational Thoughts from the Published Works of Max Lucado.* (Nashville, TN: Thomas Nelson, Inc., 2004).

8. What do we learn about being Christlike from this passage?

He says: 'My yoke is easy.' The word easy is in Greek chrēstos, which can mean well-fitting. In Palestine, ox-yokes were made of wood; the ox was brought, and the measurements were taken. The yoke was then roughed out, and the ox was brought back to have the yoke tried on. The yoke was carefully adjusted, so that it would fit well, and not chafe the neck of the patient animal. The yoke was tailor-made to fit the ox.

There is a legend that Jesus made the best ox-yokes in all Galilee, and that from all over the country people came to him to buy the best yokes that skill could make. In those days, as now, shops had their signs above the door; and it has been suggested that the sign above the door of the carpenter's shop in Nazareth may well have been: 'My yokes fit well.' It may well be that Jesus is here using a picture from the carpenter's shop in Nazareth where he had worked throughout the silent years.

Jesus says: 'My yoke fits well.' What he means is: 'The life I give you is not a burden to cause you pain; your task is made to measure to fit you.' Whatever God sends us is made to fit our needs and our abilities exactly.

Jesus says: 'My burden is light.' As a Rabbi had it: 'My burden is become my song.' It is not that the burden is easy to carry; but it is laid on us in love; it is meant to be carried in love; and love makes even the heaviest burden light. When we remember the love of God, when we know that our burden is to love God and to love one another, then the burden becomes a song. There is an old story which tells how a man came upon a little boy carrying a still smaller boy, who was lame, upon his back. 'That's a heavy burden for you to carry,' said the man. 'That's no' a burden,' came the answer. 'That's my wee brother.' The burden which is given in love and carried in love is always light. — William Barclay, *The Gospel of Matthew, Third Ed., The New Daily Study Bible* (Edinburgh: Saint Andrew Press, 2001), 20–21.

9. Matthew 12.20. What do we learn about Jesus from this verse?

In this verse from Isaiah, God is talking about Jesus. He is saying that Jesus will not break a bruised reed, meaning that Jesus does not kick us when we are down. Jesus will not snuff out a smoldering wick, meaning that Jesus does not discourage those who are barely hanging on.

God cares about people who are hurting, people who are lonely—he does not crush them. He is a gentle and merciful God who wants to help us in our sorrows.

When we are feeling small, weak and all alone, it is then that we need to go to God, and he will comfort us, lift us up and make us strong. During those lonely times God is close to us, just waiting for us to reach out to him. — Christopher D. Hudson*, NIV, Once-a-Day: At the Table*

Family Devotional, Ebook (Grand Rapids, MI: Zondervan, 2012).

10. What do we learn about being Christlike from this verse?

"Behold! My Servant.... He will not quarrel nor cry out, nor will anyone hear His voice in the streets. A bruised reed He will not break, and smoking flax He will not quench" (Matt. 12:18–20).

These words describe the pervading calmness and composure that characterized our Savior's approach to men in His work of soul-winning. Indeed, His quiet and gentle manner so impressed itself upon the mind of the Evangelist that he could not help but recall Isaiah's prophecy of Him. To Matthew, the Master's approach stood out in marked contrast to the wrangling of the Jewish scribes, the violence of the Roman officers, and even more the ravings of the false prophets and leaders of revolt such as Judas of Galilee. When confronted with broken and smoldering humanity, Jesus was tender with the broken reed and trustful with the smoking flax. This must ever be our approach if we are to succeed as soul-winners.

Writing to Timothy, the apostle Paul says, "A servant of the Lord must not quarrel but be gentle to all, able to teach, patient" (2 Tim. 2:24). — Stephen F. Olford, *The Secret of Soul-Winning* (Nashville, TN: B & H Publishing Group, 2007), 12.

11. Matthew 16.23, Luke 22.61 - 62. Does Jesus sound gentle now? What is the lesson for us in this?

As we will see, getting along is not just being nice all the time. Sometimes, we need to turn over some tables. — Josh Hunt, *How to Get Along With Almost Anyone*, 2014.

12. When is it good to be gentle and when is it time to get in someone's face?

Indeed, one of Satan's most effective plans is to lull us into ignoring conflict until it blows up into misguided confrontation. He keeps us busy, hoping the issue or person will go away. However, remaining uninvolved plays right into the hand of the enemy. To engage with another is to care. To ignore and even gossip about another is to betray. The mature follower of Christ seeks to lovingly warn others of the consequences of unwise decisions. When you take the time to confront another, you could save them from embarrassment and humiliation. They may listen, so give them a chance. Don't wait until they crash and burn, because they deserve a chance. Grace gives them an opportunity to change. Praise God for those who have offered that same grace to you.

We need each other. The Bible says, "Brothers, if someone is caught in a sin, you who are spiritual should restore him gently. But watch yourself, or you also may be tempted. Carry each other's burdens, and in this way you will fulfill the law of Christ" (Galatians 6:1-2). — Boyd Bailey, *Seeking Daily the Heart of God* (Atlanta: Wisdom Hunters, 2011).

13. Proverbs 25.15, 15.1. What benefits come to the gentle?

"A gentle answer turns away wrath, but harsh words cause quarrels" (Proverbs 15:1, TLB). Notice it says a gentle answer, not a right answer. The tone of your voice has as much to do with your success with people as anything I know. This is especially true in tense situations. You can say almost anything and get away with it if you use the right tone.

This story still sticks in my craw: I stopped to get gas at a Sam's Club a few months back. My gas tank fills from the passenger's side, but all the pumps from that side were full and had long lines. The ones on the other side were open. So I flipped a quick U-turn and came in the other way. The Gas Pump Nazi, in charge of overseeing the pumps, did not like this one bit. This was his kingdom and he wanted everyone to play by the rules. I wish I could demonstrate his body language. He came running from his throne waving his hands and screaming. "Turn around! You can't come in this way! You must go the other way!"

I did retail for a time. What they taught me was, "The customer is always right." Our friend apparently didn't attend that school.

I was pretty calm at this point. "Sir, it is a long wait going the other way. There is no one going this way. You don't want me to go to your competitor, do you?" I smiled as I spoke. "I don't care where you go, but you are not going this way!" I was shocked that he would go to the mat and give up a sale over which way people drove through the bays. I bet he wouldn't think that way if he owned the place.

I thought, "I don't want to have this conversation. I'm just going to get a little gas and go on my way." I went to grab the pump. He screams, "You can't do that!" I'm thinking, "Watch me. Who's bigger?" (Thinking, not saying, mind you.) He starts screaming, running the other way. "I will hit the emergency switch and shut down the whole place."

Wow, he's really dialed up about people driving the right direction, I thought to myself. At this point I started to imagine all the other customers looking at me angrily, so I let it go. I drove to his competitor and got some gas there.

Don't miss the point of this story. If this gentlemen had come to me with a good tone and said something like the following, I would have gladly complied: "Say, I know this is a real inconvenience. I know there's a long line for you going that way and there are no cars going this way, and it makes a lot of sense to do what you've done. I'd probably do the same thing. But my boss is really particular about this. If he were to come out here and see cars going the wrong way, he'd have my hide. Is there any chance you could pull in the other way?"

Tone is everything. A soft answer—not a right answer. — Josh Hunt, *Make Your Group Grow*, 2010.

14. Is it likely that you will EVER get a positive outcome if you use a snitty tone?

They have done research on this. What they have found is that doctors don't get sued because they make mistakes. All doctors make mistakes, but all doctors don't get sued. I have a friend who lost a baby because of a mistake by the doctor. They didn't sue. Why not? Why doesn't anyone not sue a doctor who makes a mistake?

Doctors get sued because of the tone of their voice. To test this. Psychologist Nalini Ambady listened to recordings of surgeons interacting with their patients. For each surgeon, she picked two patient conversations. Then, from each conversation, she selected two ten-second clips of the doctor talking, so her slice was a total of forty seconds. Finally, she garbled the recordings so you could not recognize individual words, but you can still discern the tone of voice. Using that slice—and that slice alone—Ambady did her analysis. She had judges rate the slices of garbled speech for such qualities as warmth, hostility, dominance, and anxiousness, and she found that by using only those ratings, she could predict which surgeons got sued and which ones didn't.35

Tone matters.

Start-up tone is especially important. The tone you use as you start the conversation will determine its outcome—with 96% accuracy. "The research shows that if your discussion begins with a harsh startup, it will inevitably end on a negative note, even if there are a lot of attempts to "make nice" in between. Statistics tell the story: 96 percent of the time you can predict the outcome of a conversation based on the first three minutes of the fifteen-minute interaction! A harsh startup simply dooms you to failure." — Josh Hunt, *How to Get Along With Almost Anyone*, 2014.

15. Let's suppose you use a gentle answer but you don't get your way. What to do then?

Some issues are not worth the fight. Or, as my daddy used to say, "That hill is not worth dying on." And as 1 Corinthians 6:7b says, "It would be far more honoring to the Lord to let yourselves be cheated" (TLB). Sure, you're right, but does it matter? Let it go!

The Gas Pump Nazi at Sam's Club was willing to die on the hill of making sure everyone entered his kingdom in the right way. If it was that important to him, he could have gotten what he wanted by using a gentle answer. Another approach would be to not die on that hill at all. Let it go.

I once heard a story of a church that just could not get this right. Every hill was worth dying on. For example, they needed a new roof for the church. Half the church wanted the roof in brown shingles, while the other half wanted it in grey shingles. Certainly an issue worth dying on, don't you think?

The "solution": They did half the roof in grey shingles and half the roof in brown shingles. It was a thoroughly ugly result. At least everyone agreed on that.

Here's another thing my dad used to say: "We don't all do things alike." This song also had a second verse: "We don't all see things alike." Variety is the spice of life. Different people do things different ways. It's all good. Sure you'd do it another way; maybe even a better way. That's OK. It's not you. It's not your deal. We don't all do things alike.

What irritates you about the people in your group? Be honest. What decisions do they make that leave you scratching your head—or shaking it?

Next question: How important is it, really? Can you place it in the file labeled "That hill is not worth dying on"?

You can measure someone's character largely by what it takes to put that person in a bad mood. Think about what sets you off, and why. And if it's not a hill worth dying on, let it go. — Josh Hunt, *Make Your Group Grow*, 2010.

16. 1 Peter 3.15. This is slightly off the main topic of today's lesson, but it is so important, I'd like us to touch on it. What reason would you give to someone who asked as to why you are a Christian? What do you love about being a Christian?

People who follow a religion through active participation in congregations tend to be happier, according to a new study.

The study by Pew Research Centre, a nonpartisan fact tank, compared the lives of religious people and non-religious people by analysing survey data from more than two dozen countries including the United States, Mexico, and Australia.

According to the results, religiously active people are typically happier and more "civically engaged" – meaning they are more likely to do things such as vote in elections or join community groups – than adults who either do not practise a religion or do not actively participate in one. https://www.independent.co.uk/life-style/religion-happy-atheism-psychology-faith-belief-emotion-mental-health-christianity-a8766376.html

17. How would you explain to someone how they could be a Christian?

Do vs. Done

This is the most simple and succinct tool I know for telling others about Christ. It gets right to the heart of the issue so many people are confused about. That is, it addresses the question of what part our own efforts play in attaining God's salvation.

Since this illustration is verbal, without need for any props or visual aids, it's a good one to use in ordinary conversations, including talks on the telephone.

It's also great for times when you know you've got to say it cleanly and quickly — like when you're on a ladder, halfway between a sailboat and a dinghy, looking up at a handful of slightly inebriated seekers! That's what I tried to do on that occasion.

"Well, first you've got to realize the difference between religion and Christianity," I started. "Religion is spelled 'D

– O,' because it consists of the things people do to try to somehow gain God's forgiveness and favor.

"But the problem is that you never know when you've done enough. It's like being a salesman who knows he must meet a quota but never being told what it is. You can never be sure that you've actually done enough. Worse yet, the Bible tells us in Romans 3:23 that we never can do enough. We'll always fall short of God's perfect standard.

"But thankfully," I went on, "Christianity is spelled differently. It's spelled 'D – O – N – E,' which means that what we could never do for ourselves, Christ has already done for us. He lived the perfect life we could never live, and He willingly died on the cross to pay the penalty we owed for the wrongs we've done.

"To become a real Christian is to humbly receive God's gift of forgiveness and to commit to following His leadership. When we do that, He adopts us into His family, and begins to change us from the inside out."

I was glad to have such a concise tool as the "Do vs. Done" illustration. Let me encourage you to master it as well. It's easy to learn, yet it's very effective as a tool to help people understand the central tenets of the Christian faith, especially those who think they can get to heaven by being good enough. — Bill Hybels and Mark Mittelberg, *Becoming a Contagious Christian* (Grand Rapids, MI: Zondervan, 2008).

18. Back to 1 Peter 3.15. What is the really important thing we need to remember when we share our faith—and all the time?

Frankly, it's here that many of us can miss the boat. The more Babylon-like our culture becomes, the more our resentment builds, resulting in bitterness, slander, rumormongering, and harsh critiques that no one would characterize as a kind and gentle rebuke.

Many excuse their words by pointing to Jesus's harsh rebukes of the Pharisees and other religious leaders of his day. But they miss the point. Jesus didn't rail on the sinners of his day. He pursued them. It was the religious hypocrites who were attempting to keep the sinners at bay that he blasted.

Nebuchadnezzar was as evil as they come. He served a demonic god. He trashed Jerusalem and God's temple. He mocked God. He was unreasonable, hotheaded, vain, murderous, and cruel.

Yet every interaction Daniel had with him was respectful and gracious. He understood that every time we treat God's enemies as our enemies, we harden their hearts and build up a wall that makes repentance all the more unlikely. — Larry Osborne, *Thriving in Babylon: Why Hope, Humility, and Wisdom Matter in a Godless Culture* (Colorado Springs, CO: David C Cook, 2015).

19. What is one arena in which you might do well to grow in gentleness?

20. How can we pray for each other this week?

Worry Less; Live More, Lesson #3
The Practice of Nearness
Good Questions Have Groups Talking
www.joshhunt.com

You might challenge your people to memorize Philippians 4.4 – 9 during this study. Nothing will drive steel in your soul like Scripture memory. Lead by example.

OPEN:

Where did you live in the 6th grade?

DIG

1. Let's review. Rejoice in the Lord always. Yes, but how?

True happiness is found in learning how to live one day at a time in spite of all the sorrow and pain life brings. It is found in learning how to rejoice in the Lord no matter what has happened in the past.

You may feel rejected or abandoned. Your faith may feel weak. Sorrow, tears, pain and emptiness may swallow you up at times, but God is still on His throne. You cannot help yourself—if only you could stop the pain and hurt. But our Lord will come to you, place His loving hand underneath you and lift you up to sit again in heavenly places.

Look up! Encourage yourself in the Lord. When the fog surrounds you and you cannot see any way out of your dilemma, lie back in the arms of Jesus and simply trust Him. He wants your faith, your confidence. He will deliver you from fear—and reveal His endless love for you! — David Wilkerson, *God Is Faithful: A Daily Invitation into the Father Heart of God* (Grand Rapids, MI: Chosen, 2012).

2. Let your gentleness be evident to all. What benefit comes to gentlemen and gentlewomen?

Lately, I've had this Bible verse chasing me around: "Let your gentleness be evident to all" (Philippians 4:5). I've run across this verse in so many unexpected places that I know it's something God wants me to pay attention to. Why? Let's just say, when the Lord was handing out the gentleness gene in July of 1969, I was apparently in another line waiting for something else. Lots of people who were being fashioned at the same time did get the gentleness gene. I know some people who I'm sure stood in line twice and got a double portion. Me? Not so much.

Now, I can have moments of gentleness. I can perform acts of gentleness. But gentleness doesn't ooze from the core of who I am. This is especially true if I am sleepy or stressed. Honestly, I think I need one of those warning signs on the bedroom door to enter at your own risk after 8:30 p.m.: "DANGER! Please note that the Holy Spirit has temporarily left this woman's body to go help a sister halfway around the world who is just now waking up."

Now, I know that is some terrible theology, but I'm being honest, y'all. What little threads of gentleness I do have are not evident past 8:30 p.m. Not. At. All.

And then there is this thing that happens when I get stressed. Normally, I can pull off a little gentleness throughout the day, but throw in a stressful situation where too much is coming at me too quickly and mercy lou! I get task-oriented and start talking in a staccato-like cadence to my people, because I want the stuff around the house done. right. now. not. in. ten. minutes. because. now. means. now!

I don't want this to be how my kids remember me. Staccato mama.

I don't want this to be how I remember me in this season of life.

So this Philippians verse that has been nipping at the edges of my heart and mind, about letting my gentleness be evident to all, is something I know I need—even if it does sting a bit.

Here's a little sermon I've been preaching to myself: Let your gentleness be evident to all. The "your" part means I do have some. Much as I'd like to believe otherwise, God didn't skip over me in distributing the gentleness gene, and my wildfire personality isn't a divine exception. Regardless of the stress I'm under, I am capable of displaying God's gentleness because the Holy Spirit is in me. I have the Holy Spirit in me when I feel all chipper at 8:30 a.m., and I have the Holy Spirit in me when I feel grumpy at 8:30 p.m. The Spirit is in me when I feel calm and when I feel stressed. Gentleness is in me! — Lysa TerKeurst, *Unglued Devotional: 60 Days of Imperfect Progress* (Nashville: Thomas Nelson, 2012).

3. Next. The Lord is near. What difference does that make?

The Lord Jesus Christ encompasses all believers with His presence (Ps. 119:151). When you have a thought, the Lord is near to read it; when you pray, the Lord is near to hear it; when you need His strength and power, He is near to provide it. In fact, He lives in you and is the source of your spiritual life. An awareness of His presence will keep you from being anxious or unstable.

Knowing the Lord is near helps us "be anxious for nothing" because we know He can handle everything we encounter. Fretting and worrying indicate a lack of trust in God. Either you've created another god who can't help you, or else you believe God could help you but refuses, which means you are questioning His integrity and Word. So delight in the Lord and meditate on His Word (Ps. 1:2). Know who He is and how He acts. Then you'll be able to say, "The Lord is near, so I'm not going to worry." — John MacArthur, *Truth for Today : A Daily Touch of God's Grace* (Nashville, Tenn.: J. Countryman, 2001), 343.

4. Preview. The Lord is near. How does this connect with what is to come?

The Lord is near! This fundamental truth provides the foundation for Philippians 4:6. You could read it this way: "The Lord is near, so do not be anxious about anything. The Lord is near, so in everything, feel comfortable about presenting your requests to him." You can go through anything; you can sit with slumped shoulders next to the hospital bedside of a loved one, facing a most fearsome future, and do so without worrying—if you are convinced the Lord is standing next to you. And he is. Philippians 4:5 tells you so.

In Philippians 4:6, prayer is mentioned three times.

The answer to anxiety and fear? Pray, pray, pray!

In Philippians 4:7, we are assured that the peace of God will chase away fear and safeguard our hearts and minds in calm-centeredness in Christ. — Joni Eareckson Tada, *Breaking the Bonds of Fear (Joni Eareckson Tada)* (Torrance, CA: Aspire Press, 2012).

5. Let's be realistic. Sometimes, it doesn't feel like God is near. What to do then?

Sometimes life can be so full of craziness and stress that we lose the sense of God's nearness. But even when we feel alienated from the Father, He is never alienated from us. Whenever we think God has moved away from us, we are mistaken; He hasn't moved at all.

God is constantly making Himself available to us, but when we become overwhelmed by the occasional distractions or inevitable disappointments of everyday life, we may be unwilling—or unable—to feel His presence or His love.

Whatever hallway you're in—no matter how long, how dark, or how scary—God is right there with you.
—Bill Hybels

The next time you feel overwhelmed by the demands of life, remember that our God isn't a distant God. He is always present; His love for you is personal, intimate, and eternal. If you genuinely desire to open your heart to the Creator, you can do so because He is not just near; He is here.

God walks with us. He scoops us up in His arms or simply sits with us in silent strength until we cannot avoid the awesome recognition that yes, even now, He is here. —

Laura Story and Thomas Nelson, *What If Your Blessings Come through Raindrops?* (Brentwood, TN: Worthy Inspired, 2012).

6. If God is near, why do so many bad things happen?

Many people today are wondering how God could allow the tragedy of September 11, 2001. What could he be thinking? Is God really in control? Can we trust him to run the universe if he would allow terrorists to take the lives of so many people?

It is important to recognize that God dwells in a different realm. He occupies another dimension. "My thoughts are not like your thoughts. Your ways are not like my ways. Just as the heavens are higher than the earth, so are my ways higher than your ways and my thoughts higher than your thoughts" (Isaiah 55:8–9).

Make special note of the word like. God's thoughts are not our thoughts, nor are they even like ours. We aren't even in the same neighborhood. We're thinking, Preserve the body; he's thinking, Save the soul. We dream of a pay raise. He dreams of raising the dead. We avoid pain and seek peace. God uses pain to bring peace. "I'm going to live before I die," we resolve. "Die so you can live," he instructs. We love what rusts. He loves what endures. We rejoice at our successes. He rejoices at our confessions. We show our children the Nike star with the million-dollar smile and say, "Be like Mike." God points to the crucified carpenter with bloody lips and a torn side and says, "Be like Christ."

Our thoughts are not like God's thoughts. Our ways are not like his ways. He has a different agenda. He dwells in a different dimension. He lives on another plane. — Max Lucado et al., Never Forget: Discovering Hope in the Aftermath of Tragedy (Nashville: Thomas Nelson, 2002).

7. Isaiah 41.10, 13 are two classics. What do we learn about God from these verses?

A favorite story of Dr. E. V. Hill tells of a young man taking a shortcut home late one evening through a vacant lot. It was dark and the shadows from the trees loomed all around him.

Suddenly he became aware of someone following him. The faster he walked, the faster the person walked. Frightened and frustrated, he turned quickly to meet his predator; but no one was there. As he turned to continue home, he heard the noise again. That was when he realized that he heard the rubbing of his corduroy pants.

We laugh at stories like this one. But the truth is, many times our fears result from imaginary thoughts, things that will never happen or come true. Satan is a relentless adversary, and he loves to fill our minds with fearful thoughts. He knows if he can frighten us enough, he will stand a good chance of paralyzing us spiritually and physically.

When you come up against a fear–producing situation, immediately pray for God's wisdom and protection, admit your inner struggle, and then stand your ground against the enemy's tactics, for God has said:

Do not fear, for I am with you;
Do not anxiously look about you, for I am your God.
I will strengthen you, surely I will help you.
(Isa. 41:10 NASB)

Charles F. Stanley, *Enter His Gates: A Daily Devotional* (Nashville: Thomas Nelson Publishers, 1998).

8. Read for application. What difference does the theology of these verses make?

A little girl and her father were returning from the funeral of their dearly loved mother and wife. Some kind neighbors invited them to spend a few days with them so they wouldn't be alone in the house with all its sad memories. However, the father decided it would be better to go home. That night the father placed the little girl's bed next to his, but neither could fall asleep. Finally the child said, "Daddy, it's dark, I can't see you. But you're there, aren't you?" "Yes, dear, Daddy's here right next to you. Go to sleep." The little one finally dropped off to sleep. In the darkness and the depth of sorrow, the father in tears said aloud, "O Heavenly Father, it's so dark, and my heart is overflowing with sorrow. But You're there, aren't You?" And immediately there came to him a passage from the prophet Isaiah: "Fear thou not; for I am with thee: be not dismayed; for I am thy God: I will strengthen thee; yea, I will help thee; I will uphold thee with the right hand of my righteousness" (Isaiah 41:10). — AMG Bible Illustrations, *Bible Illustrations Series* (Chattanooga: AMG Publishers, 2000).

9. Matthew 24.33; James 5.8. In these verses the Lord is near has to do with the fact that the Lord's coming is near. It has been 2000 years. What does it mean the coming of the Lord is near?

In the book of Revelation, Jesus made several references to His second coming, saying, "Behold, I am coming soon!" (Revelation 22:7,12,20). Almost 2000 years have passed since Jesus said this, which hardly seems soon. Scholars offer two primary suggestions of what He might have meant.

Some scholars suggest that from the human perspective it may not seem soon, but from the divine perspective,

46

it is. According to the New Testament, we have been living in the last days since Christ's incarnation (James 5:3; Hebrews 1:2). Moreover, James 5:9 states that "the Judge is standing at the door." Romans 13:12 exhorts us that "the night is far gone; the day is at hand." Hebrews 10:25 warns against "neglecting to meet together, as is the habit of some"; instead, we should be "encouraging one another, and all the more as you see the Day drawing near." And 1 Peter 4:7 warns, "The end of all things is at hand; therefore be self-controlled and sober-minded for the sake of your prayers." These verses seem to indicate that Christ is coming soon from the divine perspective.

Other scholars suggest that perhaps Jesus meant He is coming soon from the perspective of the events described in the book of Revelation. In other words, for those who will be alive during the time of the tribulation period itself—a seven-year period of trials that culminates in the second coming (see Revelation 4–19)—Christ is coming soon. — Ron Rhodes, *5-Minute Apologetics for Today: 365 Quick Answers to Key Questions* (Eugene, OR: Harvest House Publishers, Inc., 2010).

10. The Lord is coming! What difference does it make?

Jesus is coming soon to wipe away all sin and sorrow. He is coming to eradicate sin, suffer- ing, and death. He is coming to cast the devil into the lake of fire for eternity. He is coming to reward everyone according to what he has done. He is coming to reign on earth as the King of Kings and the Lord of Lords. Jesus is coming back a second time. He came to earth the first time in a humble stable—as a precious baby—destined to be a simple servant of God.

He is coming a second time boldly upon a cloud of glory, as a wise warrior of God. He will wield the word of God, leading a train of angels in worship of God and judgment. He came the first time to teach and preach that the Kingdom of God is at hand. He will come the second time to establish the Kingdom of God on earth; He gave His life during His first mission on earth. He will take life on His second mission to earth; His first coming justified our sin. His second coming will judge our sin; He submitted to kings His first time to earth. Kings will submit to Him at His Second Coming. What the disciples wanted and expected the first time will be accomplished at the Second Coming. They wanted to serve Jesus in his Kingship, but they missed a step. The Messiah had to ransom the sin of mankind first, before they could rule over mankind. As faithful followers of Jesus Christ, we invite Him to come. Soon, and very soon, we are going to see the King. We long to see our Lord. We can go to Him or He can come to us. Either way is okay. Whichever is best in His big scheme of things is what we most desire. The more time there is between his two comings, the more time we have to be about his Kingdom business.

Therefore, the promise of His Second Coming compels His followers to loving obedience. We do not want to be loafing when He returns. We do not want to be lacking in loving people when He comes back. We do not want to be embarrassed at His majestic and mighty entrance back into Earth's atmosphere. Instead, we want to be submissive to his Lordship in our individual lives. We want to model, for a lost and dying world, that we have a hope that is eternal with Him, now and forever. We want to continue our fervent prayer of, "Thy Kingdom come, on earth as it is in heaven." We want to serve the Bride of Christ, His church, with unselfish love and dedication. — Boyd Bailey, *Seeking Daily the Heart of God* (Atlanta: Wisdom Hunters, 2011).

11. Why do you look forward to the coming of Christ?

We are all part of the wedding party for Christ and His Church. The Holy Spirit is the wedding planner. God the Father is the officiator of the ceremony. Now is the rehearsal. Do you know your role? Are you dressed for the part? Are you ready for this grand and glorious processional to heaven? We will weep for the opportunity to be a part of this wondrous wedding in glory. We will weep with joy, thanksgiving, and gratitude. We will weep with excitement. We will weep when we see loved ones and saints who have gone on before us. We will weep in His presence. We will sob uncontrollably when we see His face. Our emotion will be unbridled.

Then, Jesus will quietly, lovingly, and most gently and compassionately, wipe away our tears. Our tears of sorrow will be removed, never to be seen again. We will keep our tears of joy as part of our heavenly reward. Come, Lord Jesus. Come in Your way and in Your timing. We bid You to come.

When He comes, we will be transformed and be like Him. Therefore, we can't wait. Come, Lord; we are ready. Come quickly. We can't wait. COME LORD JESUS, COME! — Boyd Bailey, *Seeking Daily the Heart of God* (Atlanta: Wisdom Hunters, 2011).

12. 2 Timothy 4.8 speaks of the reward for those who long for His appearing. Why should we long for His appearing?

ONE MORNING SEVERAL MONTHS AGO, I ROSE IN THE WEE hours and drove to Fort Campbell, Kentucky, where hundreds of people had gathered in the predawn chill to await a battalion of soldiers returning from Iraq. My close friend, Steven Pierce, was among them, and I wanted to be there to welcome him and his men home.

Steven had shipped out immediately after seeing his little boy born, and now Madden was a toddler. Others of the soldiers had never seen their children, some of whom were almost a year old. Many mothers were there, holding babies, awaiting their husbands. The troops had been away longer than expected, almost a full year.

Children, parents, grandparents, girlfriends and boyfriends, brothers and sisters—hundreds of us shivered in the cold, but without complaint. Emotions ran high because Steven's platoon had been ambushed, and the ensuing intense firefight had taken the life of one of our men, Specialist Brandon Rowe. Steven himself had been wounded in battle, and it was near-miraculous that any of the men had survived.

Now they were almost home. Over the loudspeakers came the announcement that the planes were approaching. With hundreds of others, I filed from the hangar onto the tarmac and strained to see into the darkness. A few minutes later, a shout went up, then a roar of delight. Two tiny specks, taillights blinking in the distance, approached as though in slow motion. Finally the planes rolled up to the hangar, and as the soldiers disembarked, there were shouts, cries, tears, and the popping of flashbulbs. The troops lined up in formation, and shortly afterward the words came: "Fall out!"

 Instantly the hangar became a sea of hugs, embraces, touches, and tears. If the combined emotion in that building could have been harnessed, I think it would have powered every factory in America. I've never experienced so much emotion in such a concentrated time and place, and I'll never forget it.

Only later did this thought come to me: Are we equally emotional, equally eager for our Lord's return? Are we awaiting the announcing blast of the trumpet? Casting a yearning eye to the sky? Waiting for that moment when the Lord's army will "fall out" and be "caught up"? Am I aching for that crown of righteousness which the Lord, the Righteous Judge, will award to me on that day, and to all who love His appearing?

The Apostle Paul used this title to describe the One whose Second Coming he longed for. When He does come again, Jesus will come as a righteous dispenser of justice to the world. Those of us who are His blood-bought children will have no fear, for our judgment was dispensed at Calvary. For us, it is a crown. — Robert J. Morgan, *He Shall Be Called: 150 Names of Jesus and What They Mean to You* (New York City, NY: FaithWords, 2009).

13. Philippians 1.21 – 24. How did Paul's view of Heaven affect his view of earth?

If dying and going to be with Christ is really "better by far," as Paul tells us in Philippians 1:23, why are so many Christians today afraid to die? I think the answer is that we have stored up our treasures here on Earth—and we don't want to be separated from our treasures.

Jesus commanded us, "Store up for yourselves treasures in heaven" (Matthew 6:20). His logic was that treasures on Earth won't last, and treasures in Heaven will. Hence, storing up treasures on Earth isn't just wrong, it's foolish. And storing up treasures in Heaven isn't just right, it's smart.

Tragically, many Christians store up most of their treasures on Earth. So every day that moves them closer to death moves them farther from their treasures. They end up backing into eternity, heading away from their treasures, clinging to a fallen world that hasn't been especially kind to them.

Christ calls us to turn it around—to store up our treasures in Heaven. That way, every day we get closer to our deaths, we move toward our treasures. — Randy Alcorn, *50 Days of Heaven: Reflections That Bring Eternity to Light* (Carol Stream, IL: Tyndale House Publishers, Inc., 2011).

14. I have heard people speak of some as being, "so heavenly minded they were no earthly good." Is this a danger we should be worried about? Why or why not?

If you read history you will find that the Christians who did most for the present world were just those who thought most of the next. The Apostles themselves, who set on foot the conversion of the Roman Empire, the great men who built up the Middle Ages, the English Evangelicals who abolished the Slave Trade, all left their mark on Earth, precisely because their minds were occupied with Heaven. It is since Christians have largely ceased to think of the other world that they have become so ineffective in this. Aim at Heaven and you will get earth 'thrown in': aim at earth and you will get neither. — C. S. Lewis, *Mere Christianity* (New York: HarperOne, 2001), 134.

15. Some fear Heaven will be boring. You say?

Many people think Heaven will be boring in a major way. It's too bad, but some Christians also feel that way.

People sometimes make fun of Heaven. They say, "I'd rather be having a good time in Hell than be bored in Heaven." Some imagine Hell as a place where they'll hang around, shoot pool, and joke with friends (like in Disney's Pinocchio). That is so wrong. You could hang around with friends and play and joke with them in Heaven, but not in Hell. (Remember, Satan's a liar, and some of his favorite lies are about Heaven and Hell.)

The fact is, Hell is a place where everyone is lonely and miserable, where friendship and good times don't exist. Hell will be deadly boring. Everything good, enjoyable, refreshing, fascinating, and exciting comes from God. Without God—and all the good things that come from him—there's nothing interesting to do. King David wrote, "You will show me the way of life, granting me the joy of your presence and the pleasures of living with you forever" (Psalm 16:11). Just as without God there is no joy, so in God's presence there's nothing but joy.

"Won't it be boring to be good all the time?" someone asked. This guy believed that being bad is exciting and being good is boring. But that's just a big lie. (Don't fall for it, okay?) Doing wrong things doesn't make life interesting; it makes life complicated. Sin doesn't create adventure; it creates emptiness. You may have guessed by now that my favorite book series is The Chronicles of Narnia. If you haven't read these books, I really encourage you to. Aslan the lion is the king of the fictional land Narnia just as Jesus is King of kings in the real Kingdom of Heaven. So here's my question: can you imagine Aslan ever being boring? Can you imagine anyone hanging out with Aslan who isn't totally excited to be with him?

The stories tell us "Aslan is not a tame lion." He isn't under anybody's control. Like Aslan, the real Jesus is creative, fascinating, and anything but boring. You can be sure we will always wonder what more he has waiting for us. As our leader forever, he has plans that will just blow us away! I think Heaven is going to be full of great surprises and astonishing new adventures as we learn more about God and enjoy his wonders in a new universe.

Since Heaven is God's home, made by him, it will be awesome, satisfying, and interesting, just like God is. Once we're in Heaven, we'll think we were pretty dumb not to have looked forward to it more than we did. And we'll know without a doubt that there's no place we would rather be than with our Creator, God, who is powerful but who also loves us and really wants us to be there with him! — Randy Alcorn and Linda Washington, *Heaven for Kids* (Carol Stream, IL: Tyndale House Publishers, Inc., 2012).

16. What won't be in Heaven?

There will be nothing unclean around us. We will live in a world spiritually clean from the pollution of all sin. . . . No abortion clinics, no divorce courts, no brothels, no bankruptcy courts, no psychiatric wards, and no treatment centers. . . . No pornography, no dial-a-porn, no teen suicide . . . no drive-by shootings, no racial tensions, and no prejudice.

There will be no misunderstandings, no injustice, no depression, no hurtful words, no gossip, no hurt feelings, no worry, no emptiness, and no child abuse.

There will be no wars, no financial worries . . . no heart monitors, no rust, no perplexing questions, no false teachers, no financial shortages, no hurricanes, no bad habits, no decay, no locks.

We will never need to confess sin. Never need to apologize again. Never need to straighten out a strained relationship. Never have to resist Satan again. Never have to resist temptation.

Never! — Randy Alcorn, *Eternal Perspectives: A Collection of Quotations on Heaven, the New Earth, and Life after Death* (Carol Stream, IL: Tyndale House Publishers, Inc., 2012).

17. The Lord is near can mean that Christ coming is near. But, it can also mean that God with near with us right here, right now. For some, this seems like bad news. How so?

God's nearness is bad news for those who are up to no good.

18. Why is it good news that God is near?

THE LORD IS NEAR TO ALL WHO CALL UPON HIM, TO ALL WHO CALL upon Him in truth" (v. 18). Isn't that a great promise? It's one you can put to work today. Let's look at it more closely.

First, God is near to those who are stumbling. "The LORD upholds all who fall, and raises up all who are bowed down" (v. 14). You may have stumbled and fallen. Perhaps you just didn't do what you should have. Maybe you stumbled in your job, and you are embarrassed and worried about it. Perhaps you have stumbled into sin.

Second, God is near to those who carry burdens. Those who are bowed down with the weight of care can find rest if they will call upon Him.

Third, God is near to those who are hungry. "The eyes of all look expectantly to You, and You give them their food in due season" (v. 15). Verse 16 shows how simple it is for God to answer prayer: "You open Your hand and satisfy the desire of every living thing." All God has to do is open His hand to meet our needs today. The problem is, we often don't open our hearts and cry out to Him.

Fourth, God is near to those who call upon Him. We have this great promise: "He will fulfill the desire of those who fear Him; He also will hear their cry and save them" (v. 19).

Finally, God is near to those who love Him. "The LORD preserves all who love Him, but all the wicked He will destroy" (v. 20). Follow the advice of James: "Draw near to God and He will draw near to you" (James 4:8). — Warren W. Wiersbe, Prayer, Praise & Promises: A Daily Walk through the Psalms (Grand Rapids, MI: Baker Books, 2011), 367.

19. **What do you want to remember and apply from today's study?**

20. **How can we pray for each other this week?**

Worry Less; Live More, Lesson #4
The Practice of Prayer
Good Questions Have Groups Talking
www.joshhunt.com

OPEN:

What is one thing you are grateful for today?

DIG

1. Context/ review. Philippians 4.4 – 9. What do we learn about Christian living from this passage?

We often like our information delivered to us in concise, numerical steps. In Philippians 4:4–9, the apostle Paul gives us five steps to transcendent peace:

1. Learn to rejoice in the Lord (v. 4). We can't always rejoice in our situation, but we can deliberately direct our thoughts to Him and rejoice in His presence, His promises, His power, and His providential control of all that touches us.

2. Be gentle (v. 5). Much of our anxiety comes from tension with others. We may not be able to put

out all the fires, but we can usually lower the temperature by being gentle with one another.

3. Remember the nearness of the Lord (v. 5b). The Lord is at hand, with us, near us, all around us.

4. Pray with thanksgiving (v. 6). Don't worry about anything, but pray about everything—with thanksgiving.

5. Meditate on Scripture (vv. 8–9). Let your mind think about what is true, noble, right, pure, lovely, and admirable.

This five-step formula is backed by the full authority of God, and it concludes with a double promise: The peace of God will guard our hearts and minds (v. 7), and the God of peace will be with us (v. 9). — Robert J. Morgan, *All to Jesus* (Nashville, TN: B&H Publishing Group, 2012).

2. Philippians 4.6 – 7. This is a classic, memorizable passage. Can anyone quote it from memory?

Many Christians look on the Spiritual Discipline of memorizing God's Word as something tantamount to modern-day martyrdom. Ask them to memorize Bible verses and they react with about as much eagerness as a request for volunteers to face Nero's lions. How come? Perhaps because many associate all memorization with the memory efforts required of them in school. It was work, and most of it was uninteresting and of limited value. Frequently heard, also, is the excuse of having a bad memory. But what if I offered you one thousand dollars for every verse you could memorize in the next seven days? Do you think your attitude toward Scripture memory and your ability to memorize would improve? Any financial reward would be minimal when compared to the accumulating value of the treasure of God's Word deposited within your mind. — Donald S. Whitney, *Spiritual Disciplines for the Christian Life* (Colorado Springs, CO: NavPress, 1991), 41–42.

3. What do we learn about prayer from this verse?

One of the best ways I know to remember how to commit things to God in prayer is by remembering three circles. One is the worry circle, in which I keep nothing. Second is the prayer circle, in which I keep everything. Third is the gratitude circle, in which I keep anything. So when I pray, I am anxious for nothing, prayerful for everything, and thankful for anything (Philippians 4:6).

We feel foolish asking God to help us with some of the things in our lives. But remember: "In everything by prayer and supplication, with thanksgiving, let your requests be made known to God"(Philippians 4:6). You just need to write out every one of your concerns before they turn into worries and commit them to God. He does care about each of them. If you take them back, just give them back to Him in prayer again. Day by day, as you get more and more practiced committing the affairs of your life to Him, you will begin to leave them with Him. Your trust in Him will grow, and you will stop grabbing back what you have given Him. — David Jeremiah, *Sanctuary: Finding Moments of Refuge in the Presence of God* (Nashville, TN: Integrity Publishers, 2002), 204.

4. Be anxious for nothing. What benefits come to the person who is actually able to do this?

Tom Landry, the first coach of the Dallas Cowboys football team, is one of my favorite people. When he began to coach the Cowboys, I was just getting started in my seminary program at Dallas Theological Seminary. I attended many of the weekly football luncheons and came to admire Landry as a coach and as a fellow believer in Jesus Christ. One of Coach Landry's great gifts was his ability to keep calm in the midst of battle. The TV cameras often showed him standing on the sidelines with his arms folded, seeming very relaxed, while out on the field the game was hanging in the balance. In one of his written testimonies, he revealed the secret of his composure under pressure. He said:

> Most of the athletes who fail to become winners are those athletes whose fears and anxieties prevent them from reaching their potential. I overcame my fears and anxieties by a commitment to something far greater than winning a football game—a commitment to Jesus Christ.

Landry is right! The answer to fear and anxiety is a commitment to Jesus Christ. But as we will see in this next section of Philippians, even Christians can suffer from fear and anxiety. — David Jeremiah, *Turning toward Joy* (Colorado Springs, CO: David C Cook, 2013).

5. What does worry cost us?

When worry takes over in our lives, it chokes out the Word of God (Matt. 13:7, 22). It causes us to abandon our trust in the Lord who tells us to cast all of our care upon Him (1 Peter 5:7). I read about a French soldier in World War I who carried into battle a prescription for worry:

> Of two things one is certain. Either you are at the front, or you are behind the lines. If you are at the front, of two things one is certain. Either you are exposed to danger, or you are in a safe place. If you are exposed to danger, of two things one is certain. Either you are wounded, or you are not wounded. If you are wounded, of two things one is certain. Either

you recover, or you die. If you recover, there is no need to worry. If you die, you can't worry.

While that seems like a rather fatalistic approach to the problem, it coincides with numerous studies that have been done on the subject. Forty percent of the things people worry about never happen. Thirty percent of the worries are related to past matters which are now beyond the patients' control. Twelve percent have to do with anxiety about health even though there is no illness except in the imagination. Ten percent is worry about friends, or neighbors, even though in most cases, there is no reason for their anxiety. Just 8 percent of the worries seemed to have some basis in reality. What this means is that 90 percent of the things we worry about never happen! — David Jeremiah, *Turning Toward Joy* (Colorado Springs, CO: David C Cook, 2013).

6. What is God's part, and what is our part of living worry-free lives?

The worrisome heart pays a high price for doing so. Worry comes from the Greek word that means "to divide the mind." Anxiety splits us right down the middle, creating a double-minded thinker. Rather than take away tomorrow's trouble, worry voids today's strength. Perception is divided, distorting your vision. Strength is divided, wasting your energy. Who can afford to lose power?

But how can we stop doing so? Paul offers a two-pronged answer: God's part and our part. Our part includes prayer and gratitude. "Don't worry about anything; instead, pray about everything. Tell God what you need, and thank him for all he has done" (Phil. 4:6 NLT, emphasis mine).

God's part? "If you do this, you will experience God's peace, which is far more wonderful than the human mind can understand" (Phil. 4:7 NLT). — *Come Thirsty* / Max Lucado, *Grace for the Moment® Volume Ii: More Inspirational Thoughts for Each Day of the Year* (Nashville: Thomas Nelson, 2006).

7. We have all kinds of reasons to be anxious. What do we know about Paul's audience? What reasons did they have to be anxious?

Because of their status as citizens of a Roman colony, the Philippian Christians were certainly candidates for anxiety. The persecution from Nero was beginning to boil and the effects were starting to be felt all over the Roman domain. These young Christians knew that they would soon be tested for their walk with God. — David Jeremiah, *Turning Toward Joy* (Colorado Springs, CO: David C Cook, 2013).

8. Do not be anxious. What does it mean to be anxious? How would you define it?

The New Testament word for worry is translated "take thought" and "be careful" in the Authorized Version. The word worry comes from the Greek word merimnao which is a combination of two words: merizo, which means "to divide," and nous, which means "mind." So to worry is to have a mind divided between legitimate thoughts and destructive thoughts. No wonder James says that a double-minded man is "unstable in all his ways" (James 1:8).

The word "anxious" that Paul uses is a synonym for our word "worry." It is the same word that Jesus used when He told Martha that she was "worried and troubled about many things" (Luke 10:41). Our Lord also used this word in talking with His disciples when He told them that they were to "take no thought" about food, drink, clothing, or shelter (Matt. 6:25). Obviously He was not suggesting that they should never think about such things; rather, He was reminding them that they should not worry about them. — David Jeremiah, *Turning Toward Joy* (Colorado Springs, CO: David C Cook, 2013).

9. Do not be anxious, instead, pray. This is a classic case of the principle of replacement. Replace worry with prayer. Overcome evil with good. Take off the old; put on the new. Why is this better than just trying hard not to worry?

I remember a time when this happened to me. When I woke up one morning, I immediately thought about what Jim (not his real name) had done to me the previous day. Since I had forgiven him, I tried to stop to thinking about it. Within fifteen minutes, however, the same thoughts were rolling through my mind. I pushed them aside once more, but before long, there they were again. After wrestling with these painful thoughts several more times, I realized I was stuck in a rut. When I asked God to change my heart and help me get rid of these thoughts and feelings, these two Bible passages came to my mind:

"But I tell you who hear me: Love your enemies, do good to those who hate you, bless those who curse you, pray for those who mistreat you" (Luke 6:27–28).

> "Finally, brothers, whatever is true, whatever is noble, whatever is right, whatever is pure, whatever is lovely, whatever is admirable—if anything is excellent or praiseworthy—think about such things" (Phil. 4:8).

"Okay," I prayed, "but I'll need your help, Lord. I sure don't feel like doing any of this." By God's grace, I began to pray for Jim, asking God to be with him and to bless his day. My thoughts then turned to other matters. When I caught myself thinking about the offense an hour later, I prayed for Jim again, this time thanking God for some of Jim's admirable qualities. This process repeated itself many times during the next two days, and then I discovered something amazing. Whenever Jim came to my mind, my thoughts were usually positive and no longer gravitated toward the offense he had committed.

This was how I learned the replacement principle. It is very difficult simply to stop thinking about an unpleasant experience. Instead, we must replace negative thoughts and memories with positive ones. This principle is especially helpful when trying to keep the first promise of forgiveness. Every time you begin to dwell on or brood over what someone has done, ask for God's help and deliberately pray for that person or think of something about the offender that is "true, noble, right, pure, lovely, admirable, excellent, or praiseworthy." At first, you may struggle to come up with even one positive thought, but after you find one good thought or memory, others should come more easily. If you cannot think of a single good thing about the person you are trying to forgive, then use thankful thoughts about God and his work in this situation to replace unpleasant memories (see Phil. 4:4–7). — Ken Sande, *The Peacemaker: A Biblical Guide to Resolving Personal Conflict, Third Edition*. (Grand Rapids, MI: Baker Books, 2004), 220–221.

10. By prayer and petition. What is the difference between prayer and petition?

The way to remain in the place of rejoicing, the way to avoid being caught up in extravagance of any sort is to remain in prayer. In this context, prayer refers to communing with God, while supplication speaks of making specific requests to Him. Both are to be done with a spirit of thanksgiving for the abundance with which the Lord has already blessed us both materially and spiritually (Psalm 68:19). — Jon Courson, *Jon Courson's Application Commentary* (Nashville, TN: Thomas Nelson, 2003), 1292.

11. What is prayer? How would you define it?

The older I get, the more I'm learning that prayer is not a monologue. It's a dialogue. I'm discovering more and more that the real need in my life is not for God to hear from me, but for me to hear from Him. And I find that as I walk, drive, or get on my knees, if I will pray a phrase or two and then just rest and be quiet, the Lord will bring specific scriptures to my mind or will write His will upon my heart concerning how I am to pray.

But if I pray sentence after paragraph after page and then say, "Okay, that wraps it up for prayer time today," I really miss it. Oh, I know that even that kind of prayer has power. Any prayer is better than no prayer. But I suggest that if you learn to pause and listen in prayer, the Lord will show you how to believe on behalf of another, and how to pray specifically concerning any given situation. — Jon Courson, *Jon Courson's Application Commentary* (Nashville, TN: Thomas Nelson, 2003), 1292.

12. Does God always answer prayer? Always?

"That's easy for Paul," you say. "His prayers were always answered the way he wanted."

Really? Check out what he said to the Romans...

Now I beseech you, brethren, for the Lord Jesus Christ's sake, and for the love of the Spirit, that ye strive together with me in your prayers to God for me; that I may be delivered from them that do not believe in Judaea; and that my service which I have for Jerusalem may be accepted of the saints; that I may come unto you with joy by the will of God, and may with you be refreshed. Romans 15:30–32

As he comes to the end of his letter to the Romans, Paul says, "Pray with me—first that I may be delivered from my enemies in Jerusalem; second, that my service may be accepted by the Christians; and finally, that I may come to you at Rome with joy."

But what happened? Paul was captured by his enemies in Jerusalem. His ministry was not readily accepted by the saints. And the only way he made it to Rome was as a prisoner.

Here's the deal, gang: God can say "Yes" to my prayers, or He can say "No." Either way, it's an answer. How many, many times I have said, "Here's my supplication, Father..." only to see that, down the road, what takes place is a whole lot better than what I asked for. — Jon Courson, *Jon Courson's Application Commentary* (Nashville, TN: Thomas Nelson, 2003), 1295–1296.

13. Is anything too big to pray about? Is anything too small?

Paul stresses that we can take everything to God in prayer. As it has been beautifully put, 'There is nothing too great for God's power; and nothing too small for his fatherly care.' Children may take anything, great or small, to their parents, sure that whatever happens to them is of interest there, their small triumphs and disappointments, their passing cuts and bruises. In exactly the same way, we may take anything to God, sure of his interest and concern. — William Barclay, *The Letters to Philippians, Colossians, and Thessalonians, 3rd ed. fully rev. and updated., The New Daily Study Bible* (Louisville, KY; London: Westminster John Knox Press, 2003), 90.

14. With thanksgiving. Why do you think God led Paul to include this?

In his biography of Sidlow Baxter, E. A. Johnston relates a story about this verse. When Baxter was eighty-eight, he preached in Memphis, saying, "I was over in Scotland and at one point while there I slumped into a deep despondency. Everything seemed upsetting and frustrating and foreboding. . . . It seemed as though the promises of the Bible were like pie crust. Was it any use praying longer? I was having trouble with deafness. And along with that, tinnitus. Loud noises in both my ears day and night. . . . I went to bed weary with mental wrestling and frustration. And then, somewhere between night and morning, September 6th and 7th, something happened that changed everything. I heard no audible voice but someone had wakened me amid the curtains of the night; and was speaking within me. . . . He said, 'Sid! Sid! Are you forgetting Philippians 4, verses 6 and 7?' Those verses 6 and 7 perfectly match September 6 and 7. 'You've been forgetting the thanksgiving. Hand everything over to Me, Sid. And start praying again with thanksgiving. And start believing that what you ask for becomes yours. TRY IT, Sid. And if you do, Philippians 4:6 and 7 is all yours.'"

Baxter continued: "Philippians 4:6 and 7 was like an electric bulb turned on. And I saw everything with illuminating difference and clearness. . . . My whole nervous system had become relaxed. And as I prayed with thanksgiving—I could never forget it—the peace of God invaded my heart like a gentle zephyr." — Robert J. Morgan, *100 Bible Verses Everyone Should Know by Heart* (Nashville, TN: B&H Publishing Group, 2010).

15. What other verses can you think of—or find—that speak to the importance of gratitude?

God is not giving us this attitude because He hopes we'll have it in heaven. Thanksgiving here on earth is not an option. It is very clear in the New Testament that ingratitude is sin.

In the first chapter of Romans, when Paul is cataloguing the destruction of a culture, he says one of the evidences of the decadence of human society is that people become unthankful. In Timothy he gives as one of the evidences of the end times that people are unthankful.

In the story of the ten lepers, nine of the lepers that Jesus healed walked away without saying, "Thank you." Only one gave Him thanks. The Lord was not happy with the other nine. When we don't have a spirit of gratitude, we violate the Word of God.

If you are not a thankful person, you are out of God's will. 1 Thessalonians 5:18 says, "In everything give thanks; for this is the will of God in Christ Jesus for you." There are a lot of things we don't know for sure concerning the will of God. You have to pull those principles together and try to determine what God wants you to do. But one thing I know, it is the will of God for you to be thankful. When you choose to be ungrateful, you have moved your life out of that circle of God's perfect will.

Second, if you are not thankful, you are out of peace with God. We live in a day of great distress, depression and despair. But God has the answer to that in His Word. He tells us in Philippians 4 that we are to "be anxious for nothing...." That means don't let anxiety take over in your life. "But in everything by prayer and supplication, with thanksgiving, let your requests be made know to God; and the peace of God, which surpasses all understanding, will guard your hearts and minds through Christ Jesus" (vv. 6–7). — David Jeremiah, *Fruit of the Spirit: Study Guide* (Nashville, TN: Thomas Nelson Publishers, 1995), 122–123.

16. What benefits do the grateful enjoy?

Ruth Bell Graham once told of laying awake at three o'clock in another country, worried about someone she loved who was trying hard to run away from God. As she later recalled, "Suddenly the Lord said to me, 'Quit studying the problems and start studying the promises.' Now God has never spoken to me audibly, but there is no mistaking when He speaks. So I turned on the light, got out my Bible, and the first verse that came to me was Philippians 4:6."

The two words that struck her were these: with thanksgiving.

"Suddenly I realized the missing ingredient in my prayers had been 'with thanksgiving.' So I put down my Bible and spent time worshipping Him for who He is and what He is. . . . I began to thank God for giving me this one I loved so dearly in the first place. I even thanked Him for the difficult spots which taught me so much. And you know what happened? It was as if suddenly someone turned on the lights in my mind and heart, and the little fears and worries which, like mice and cockroaches, had been nibbling away in the darkness, suddenly scuttled for cover." — Robert J. Morgan, *100 Bible Verses Everyone Should Know by Heart* (Nashville, TN: B&H Publishing Group, 2010).

17. How does my gratitude benefit the people around me?

A man who was on the verge of a nervous breakdown was counseled to practice the therapy of thanksgiving. He was told to make a list of all the people who had ever helped him in his life. Then he was to sit down and write a letter of thanks to a person who had especially blessed his life in the past. This man thought through his life and remembered a school teacher he'd had when he was growing up. She was a very old lady now. He wrote her a letter expressing his appreciation for all she'd meant to his life during his days of schooling.

Several days went by and he got a letter back from her. She wrote, "Dear Willie, as I recall all the children I have taught over the years, you are the only one who ever took time to write and thank me for what I did as a teacher. You've made me so happy. I've read your letter through tears. I keep it by my bedside and read it every night. I shall cherish it until the day I die."

This man was so thrilled by the reply that he wrote more letters. At last he'd written 500 letters to the people he felt grateful to. You know what happened? The man got better. — David Jeremiah, *Fruit of the Spirit: Study Guide* (Nashville, TN: Thomas Nelson Publishers, 1995), 123–124.

18. The peace of God will guard your hearts and minds. What exactly does that mean?

What does this mean? The word guard was a military term that described a Roman soldier holding his weapon, walking back and forth in front of an open gate so that no one could enter. Paul is saying that this is how God will guard your hearts and give you His peace. Our Father is a Father who delights to give good gifts to His children. He will actively guard your heart against whatever is troubling it. He will not allow any menacing worry to enter.

This verse commands us to ask for anything and guarantees an answer. First, we may get what we ask for, because He delights in giving us gifts, but no matter what the outcome, He definitely promises to give us His peace. This means that if we don't get what we asked for, we've got something better—satisfaction. Our hearts will be satisfied with or without our initial request, regardless of what was troubling us to begin with. — *The Priority of Knowing God*, Peter V. Deison, 1990 Discovery House, p. 56 / Galaxie Software, *10,000 Sermon Illustrations* (Biblical Studies Press, 2002).

19. What do you want to remember and apply from today's study?

20. How can we pray for each other this week?

Worry Less; Live More, Lesson #5
The Practice of Thanksgiving
Good Questions Have Groups Talking
www.joshhunt.com

OPEN:

What is one thing that is on your mind these days?

DIG

1. **Philippians 4.6 – 7. With thanksgiving. We touched on this last week and will dig in this week. What is thanksgiving? How would you define it?**

    Thanksgiving is just what the word itself signifies—the giving of thanks to God. It is giving something to God in words which we feel at heart for blessings received. Gratitude arises from a contemplation of the goodness of God. It is bred by serious meditation on what God has done for us. Both gratitude and thanksgiving point to, and have to do with God and His mercies. The heart is consciously grateful to God. The soul gives expression to that heartfelt gratitude to God in words or acts. — Edward M. Bounds, *The Essentials of Prayer* (Grand Rapids, MI: Christian Classics Ethereal Library, 2004), 18.

2. **What is the opposite of gratitude?**

    Gratitude and thanksgiving forever stand opposed to all murmurings at God's dealings with us, and all complainings at our lot. Gratitude and murmuring never abide in the same heart at the same time. An unappreciative spirit has no standing beside gratitude and praise. And true prayer corrects complaining and promotes gratitude and thanksgiving. Dissatisfaction at one's lot, and a disposition to be discontented with things which come to us in the providence of God, are foes to gratitude and enemies to thanksgiving.

The murmurers are ungrateful people. Appreciative men and women have neither the time nor disposition to stop and complain. The bane of the wilderness-journey of the Israelites on their way to Canaan was their proneness to murmur and complain against God and Moses. For this, God was several times greatly grieved, and it took the strong praying of Moses to avert God's wrath because of these murmurings. The absence of gratitude left no room nor disposition for praise and thanksgiving, just as it is so always. But when these same Israelites were brought through the Red Sea dry shod, while their enemies were destroyed, there was a song of praise led by Miriam, the sister of Moses. One of the leading sins of these Israelites was forgetfulness of God and His mercies, and ingratitude of soul. This brought forth murmurings and lack of praise, as it always does.
— Edward M. Bounds, *The Essentials of Prayer* (Grand Rapids, MI: Christian Classics Ethereal Library, 2004), 19.

3. How are prayer, praise and thanksgiving related?

PRAYER, praise and thanksgiving all go in company. A close relationship exists between them. Praise and thanksgiving are so near alike that it is not easy to distinguish between them or define them separately. The Scriptures join these three things together. Many are the causes for thanksgiving and praise. The Psalms are filled with many songs of praise and hymns of thanksgiving, all pointing back to the results of prayer. Thanksgiving includes gratitude. In fact thanksgiving is but the expression of an inward conscious gratitude to God for mercies received. Gratitude is an inward emotion of the soul, involuntarily arising therein, while thanksgiving is the voluntary expression of gratitude.

Thanksgiving is oral, positive, active. It is the giving out of something to God. Thanksgiving comes out into the open. Gratitude is secret, silent, negative, passive, not showing its being till expressed in praise and thanksgiving. Gratitude is felt in the heart. Thanksgiving is the expression of that inward feeling. — Edward M. Bounds, *The Essentials of Prayer* (Grand Rapids, MI: Christian Classics Ethereal Library, 2004), 18.

4. We all know we should be grateful. What action steps can we take to turn wishful thinking into reality?

Gratitude is born of meditation on God's grace and mercy. "The Lord hath done great things for us, whereof we are glad." Herein we see the value of serious meditation. "My meditation of him shall be sweet." Praise is begotten by gratitude and a conscious obligation to God for mercies given. As we think of mercies past, the heart is inwardly moved to gratitude.

"I love to think on mercies past,
And future good implore;
And all my cares and sorrows cast
On Him whom I adore."

Edward M. Bounds, *The Essentials of Prayer* (Grand Rapids, MI: Christian Classics Ethereal Library, 2004), 18.

5. **Much of life—indeed, most of life—is habit. What can we do to turn gratitude into an unstoppable habit?**

It is good to praise the LORD . . ., proclaiming your love in the morning and your faithfulness at night. PSALM 92:1– 2

We develop some habits at such a young age that we barely notice them today. Brushing teeth, combing hair, and washing hands are taught repeatedly to children until they're well-established habits. Throughout life, we develop more habits, both good and bad. Daily exercise, emotional eating, addiction, saving money, spending money recklessly, saying please and thank you, avoiding conflict—these habits are all formed over time.

We form cognitive habits, too, like gratitude. Imagine the difference this could make in your daily life. If instead of being frustrated that a meeting ran late, you were thankful for the innovative ideas that were shared. If you soaked in the tenderness of comforting a crying baby at 2:00 a.m. without despairing over lost sleep. Gratitude can change your outlook—and actions—in life-changing ways. It takes practice and some failures; habits don't develop overnight. But by choosing gratitude moment by moment, you'll see it become second nature. — Thomas Nelson, *100 Days of Thanks* (Nashville: Thomas Nelson, 2018).

6. **What about when life is hard… how can we be grateful then?**

Gratitude to God can be a moment-by-moment expression. Even in the middle of the worst of circumstances, your thanksgiving to God is appropriate and needed. Look beyond your current condition to your heavenly hope. He has prepared a place for you, and His preparations are not lacking. They are just what you need and desire. So, your thanksgiving is for what He has done in the past, His current provision, and what He has prepared for you in the future. God's generosity is without competition. You can be very, very grateful for this. Let thanksgiving escape from your lips often. Use it to put out the fires of fear and worry before they spread too far. Thanks be to God, for you are made rich. Yes, in Christ you are made rich. You have everything needed for this life in Christ. As a consequence of your management of His riches, you can be ridiculously generous. This is the natural result of thanksgiving. Because of your deep gratitude to God, you are called and compelled to give. Gratitude invites you to generosity. You cannot experience authentic thanksgiving and not see it birth giving. It is a beautiful process: because God has given to you, you give to others. At the moment you receive the gift of God, generosity is conceived in your heart. — Boyd Bailey, *Seeking Daily the Heart of God* (Atlanta: Wisdom Hunters, 2011).

7. Here is a question I ask often. I ask it often because it is so important. Why benefits come to the grateful?

Love is the child of gratitude. Love grows as gratitude is felt, and then breaks out into praise and thanksgiving to God: "I love the Lord because he hath heard my voice and my supplication." Answered prayers cause gratitude, and gratitude brings forth a love that declares it will not cease praying: "Because he hath inclined his ear unto me, therefore will I call upon him as long as I live." Gratitude and love move to larger and increased praying.

Paul appeals to the Romans to dedicate themselves wholly to God, a living sacrifice, and the constraining motive is the mercies of God:

"I beseech you, therefore, brethren, by the mercies of God, that ye present your bodies a living sacrifice, holy, acceptable unto God, which is your reasonable service."

Consideration of God's mercies not only begets gratitude, but induces a large consecration to God of all we have and are. So that prayer, thanksgiving and consecration are all linked together inseparably. — Edward M. Bounds, *The Essentials of Prayer* (Grand Rapids, MI: Christian Classics Ethereal Library, 2004), 18–19.

8. What keeps us from the grateful life?

Keep your eyes open, hold tight to your convictions, give it all you've got, be resolute, and love without stopping.
1 CORINTHIANS 16:13–14 MSG

You've probably heard the phrase, "It's the journey, not the destination." That sentiment is directly applicable to the theme of gratitude. Picture two runners on identical courses. Their goal is the finish line, but their time isn't important; they're running for the enjoyment of the sport. One runner dashes off, her eyes focused on the next mile, then the next, and the next. She is efficient, oblivious to everything but the end. As she sprints forward, her surroundings blur. The other runner knows the course is short and wants to experience it all. She looks around, noticing the brilliant blue sky. She sees familiar faces cheering her on and feels the gentle breeze, soaking it all in. She is present and grateful.

If we go through the day without feeling thankful for anything, it's because we're too focused on the finish line. We aren't looking at the gifts around us. We aren't being present. Life is short. Look up, make eye contact, experience the gifts all around you, and enjoy the run.

Remember: it's the journey, not the destination. — Thomas Nelson, *100 Days of Thanks* (Nashville: Thomas Nelson, 2018).

9. **Let's explore some things we have to be grateful for. First, life on planet earth. Psalms 19.1 says that the heavens declare the glory of God. Let's think specifically about living where we live. What do you love about living here?**

When I consider Your heavens, the work of Your fingers, the moon and the stars, which You have ordained; . . . O LORD, our Lord, how majestic is Your name in all the earth! PSALM 8:3, 9 NASB

Delicate crocuses push through frozen ground; autumn leaves cast a golden hue; foam-tipped waves flash in the sunlight. Does God's creation leave you breathless? Even on the coldest and darkest days, stars shimmer. Giant redwoods stand majestic. God could have created this world to merely be workable, practical. He could have stopped with one type of tree and flower. But He chose to encompass the universe with vast beauty to delight us daily. Praise our loving and gracious Creator! — Thomas Nelson, *100 Days of Thanks* (Nashville: Thomas Nelson, 2018).

10. **I am grateful for God. I am grateful for God just the way He is. Let's think about that. Theologians call this field of study the attributes of God. Let's list some attributes. What attributes of God are you grateful for?**

"The LORD, the LORD God, compassionate and gracious, slow to anger, and abounding in lovingkindness and truth." EXODUS 34:6 NASB

God's gifts reflect His character. He is full of grace, compassionate, faithful, all-powerful, merciful, and wise. He is patient, kind, and gentle. Did you see a sick friend begin to heal? God is all-powerful. Did you feel His deep and abiding presence during a low point this week? God is compassionate. Maybe you experienced His forgiveness after deliberately choosing not to obey His Word. God is merciful. Praise the Lord for His perfect character. — Thomas Nelson, *100 Days of Thanks* (Nashville: Thomas Nelson, 2018).

11. Psalm 139.13ff suggests that we should be thankful for the way God has made us. Are you thankful how God has made you—your body, your talents and so forth? How so? Does this sound egotistical? What do you love about being you?

After this I looked, and there before me was a great multitude that no one could count, from every nation, tribe, people and language, standing before the throne and before the Lamb. They were wearing white robes and were holding palm branches in their hands. And they cried out in a loud voice: "Salvation belongs to our God, who sits on the throne, and to the Lamb." REVELATION 7:9–10

Our world holds 7.6 billion people,1 each with different fingerprints, ear shapes, irises, voices, and gaits. Our stories, talents, personalities, creativity, humor, leadership skills, and idiosyncrasies make each of us unique. The world would be monotonous with 7.6 billion clones, wouldn't it? Thankfully God loves diversity. He created a world of different races, languages, customs, and cultures; the differences are beautiful, and they challenge and pull us out of our comfort zones. Thank God for the diverse creation He created. — Thomas

Nelson, *100 Days of Thanks* (Nashville: Thomas Nelson, 2018).

12. Another source of gratitude is the people in our lives. Who are you grateful for? How so?

I thank my God every time I remember you. PHILIPPIANS 1:3

Do you have a memory of a stranger, acquaintance, or someone else you didn't know well having a positive impact on your life? Do you remember your kindergarten teacher instructing you on how to read? Or a soccer coach who believed in you—even when you didn't? What about a pastor, therapist, neighbor, or camp counselor? Every relationship, whether for a season or a lifetime, is a unique facet of your life's story. Think about how one of these people, even though he or she may have only briefly crossed paths with you, blessed your life in some way. — Thomas Nelson, *100 Days of Thanks* (Nashville: Thomas Nelson, 2018).

13. How can you be grateful for people when they drive you crazy? Do people ever drive you crazy?

A FRIEND WHO IS SELF-EMPLOYED AS A GRAPHIC ARTIST told me he was having a bad day—so terrible, in fact, that he was contemplating giving up his freelance career for a nine-to-five job.

Was he sick of graphic design? No, he said, he still liked doing the work, but the people were driving him crazy. "This would be a great business if it weren't for the clients," he commented grimly.

Wrong. If it weren't for the clients and customers, you and I and everyone else in business would be out of business. In fact, pleasing customers is the sole reason our companies (whether we own them or are employed by someone else) exist.

Can people be difficult to deal with? Absolutely. Can customers give us grief? Of course. But our prosperity depends on satisfying enough customers often enough to keep us in business.

One thing that has helped me is to realize that people don't mean to be mean. They're not intentionally difficult or rude. It's just that folks are so busy, and have so much to do, that when there is a problem or delay, they blow their stack. Put yourself in the customer's shoes. If your car wasn't ready when it was supposed to be . . . if the steak was rare instead of well-done as you requested . . . would you be upset? Well, then don't be shocked when your customers complain. After all, they're only human.

I know lots of people who say, "I hate clients." Well, I love my clients! They give me the opportunity to do the work I enjoy and earn a living so I can take care of my family. Without customers, you don't have a business.

In his best-selling book, Think and Grow Rich, Napoleon Hill said that "a positive mental attitude" and "a pleasing personality" are the two most effective tools for dealing effectively with people in business. They will make customers happy. And when your customers are happy, you reap the rewards. — Robert W. Bly, *Count Your Blessings: 63 Things to Be Grateful for in Everyday Life . . . and How to Appreciate Them* (Nashville: Thomas Nelson, 2008).

14. I am thankful for the Bible. I am sure you are as well. What do you love about the Bible?

Your word is a lamp for my feet, a light on my path.
PSALM 119:105

It's remarkable the Bible still has relevancy in our modern age of electric cars and video chatting. Though times have changed, the Lord's Word continues to be a light to our every footstep. Its promises bring comfort and hope, it equips us to serve, and its truth renews our minds. It is an invaluable and irreplaceable gift. — Thomas Nelson, *100 Days of Thanks* (Nashville: Thomas Nelson, 2018).

15. Bible promises. What are some of your favorites? What biblical promises are you grateful for?

You intended to harm me, but God intended it for good to accomplish what is now being done, the saving of many lives.

GENESIS 50:20

It's easy—effortless, even—to have a grateful heart during the happy times, when you're overcome with God's goodness. When you're offered your dream job, repair a broken relationship, or see a loved one healed, rejoicing comes easily. Bad news brings a different reaction. You feel discouraged, fearful, angry, sad, and a threshold of other challenging emotions. You might feel, as the psalmist says in Psalm 119:28, your "soul is weary with sorrow." How can you be grateful in trying times? Is it even possible?

We don't have easy answers; we may not understand until we are with the Lord. But we know and cling to this truth: our pain will not be wasted. Romans 8:28

reminds us, "God causes all things to work together for good" (NASB). Not just some things, but all things—the good and the bad. You can be comforted, you can even give thanks and rejoice, because the pain will cease. God has already written the end of the story. And it all works together for good. — Thomas Nelson, *100 Days of Thanks* (Nashville: Thomas Nelson, 2018).

16. What physical things are you grateful for? Cars. Computers. TVs. Indoor plumbing. Let's make a list—a long list.

AS A COLD-WEATHER ENTHUSIAST, I BELIEVE THE WORLD becomes nearly uninhabitable for three months out of every year—namely, summer. And every summer, I close the windows, turn down the thermostat, and thank God for air-conditioning, without which my life would be absolutely miserable during the summer months.

Although the first commercial air conditioner, built by Willis H. Carrier, was an industrial unit installed in a Brooklyn printing plant in 1902, room air conditioners didn't start making it into homes until the 1960s. So I am old enough to remember living in a house without air-conditioning. Can you imagine never being able to get cool and comfortable? That was the way things were in summer.

A friend relates: "We lived in an apartment in the Bronx, and my father worked evenings. I remember him trying to sleep during the day in the summer. The bed would be soaked with sweat, and he would wrap himself with wet towels trying to get cool." Sheer torment.

An air conditioner is like a refrigerator, except it cools the air outside the box instead of inside. The secret is Freon, a refrigerant that makes an endless transition from gas to liquid and back to gas again as it is cycled through the unit.

Like all liquids, Freon absorbs heat as it becomes a gas. Heat is absorbed from the air, cooling it. As the air cools, it gives off moisture. The moisture condenses, which is why you always see water dripping from air conditioners sticking out of walls and windows.

We often take blessings like air-conditioning for granted— until we don't have them. As I write this, we have just emerged from the most intense heat wave of this summer, which turned most of New Jersey into a steam bath. And we just moved into a new house, in which the central air-conditioning picked this week to fail.

All of us were moaning and groaning. The kids and I complained about the heat; my wife, about the expense of replacing the unit.

Without air-conditioning, the quality of my life was severely compromised. I couldn't sleep, so I was tired the next day and unproductive at work. I couldn't even get close to comfortable in my own home, so I couldn't enjoy simple leisure activities we take for granted, such as reading or watching TV.

But thank God we have the money to buy a new air conditioner. Thank God there is such a thing as an air conditioner to buy.

The installer is almost finished hooking up the unit. Excuse me for a minute while I turn the thermostat down to sixty-eight and indulge my passion for keeping cool. — Robert W. Bly, *Count Your Blessings: 63 Things to Be Grateful for in Everyday Life . . . and How to Appreciate Them* (Nashville: Thomas Nelson, 2008).

17. I am grateful to be an American, how about you? What do you love about living in America?

"God bless America," the old song says. And repopularized in the wake of the tragic terrorist attacks on the World Trade Center and the Pentagon of September 11, 2001, a more contemporary song exclaims: "I'm proud to be an American!" If there is one good thing to come out of 9-11, it is a renewed national spirit of patriotism and a nationwide appreciation of the privilege we enjoy living in the greatest country in the world.

As one anonymous author observes:

What does it mean to be an American? If you ask any of the more than 280 million citizens of the United States, chances are you will get more than 280 million unique answers. But they all will have one common thread running through them—that to be an American is to be free.

Which leads to the question, What is freedom? Most Americans will say that freedom is the opportunity to make choices based upon their values, goals, and desires. Some might say it's the chance to be whoever they want to be. Still others might suggest it is the ability to speak their mind without worry of retribution. Freedom means many things to many people, yet we often neglect to think about what it means to us until there is a threat of it being taken away.

Terrorist actions, war, martial law—these things run rampant in many troubled nations, yet America has had very little experience with challenges to the day-to-day freedoms we exercise without a second thought.

Think about how blessed we are as a nation, as a people, to be free. Free to think, act, speak, and dream with no limitations to what we can accomplish. But in order to keep the freedoms we hold so dear, we must never take them for granted. Honoring and fighting for freedom both here and the world over—that is what it means to be an American. — Robert W. Bly, *Count Your Blessings: 63 Things to Be Grateful for in Everyday Life . . . and How to Appreciate Them* (Nashville: Thomas Nelson, 2008).

18. 2 Timothy 4.13 (Living) "Don't forget the books." Books have always been important to the people of God. What good Christian books are you grateful for?

A BOOK THAT INSTRUCTS IN SOME PROFITABLE FIELD is a priceless treasure. It stands patient and mute until you command it to teach. When it teaches, it teaches only as fast as you are capable of learning, and will repeat the difficult parts as often as is necessary to firmly entrench them in your brain. It will never rebuke you for tardiness to class, nor complain under a thousand interruptions. It never forgets even a minor principle of its conceptual message, yet it will not scold you if you forget even major ones. Such a book ranks with a faithful hound as one of man's best friends. If the bookseller offers it and you pass up the chance of ownership, who suffers the most: You? Or the bookseller, who will only sell it to the next one who browses? —JERRY BUCHANAN

I confess: I'm a bookworm. A bibliophile. A bookaholic. I love books. Always have, always will. Which is why I'm grateful they're still around—and that the Internet has not yet wiped them off the face of the earth....

So, my kids can escape the pressures of life with video games or by watching TV. As for me, I'd rather curl up with a good book and read as the world passes me by.

— Robert W. Bly, *Count Your Blessings: 63 Things to Be Grateful for in Everyday Life . . . and How to Appreciate Them* (Nashville: Thomas Nelson, 2008).

19. **One last category: music. What worship songs are you grateful for? What does music do for you? What do you love about music?**

    Martin Luther said, "The devil takes flight at the sound of music, just as he does at the words of theology, and for this reason the prophets always combined theology and music, the teaching of truth and the chanting of Psalms and hymns." "After theology, I give the highest place and greatest honor to music." — Galaxie Software, *10,000 Sermon Illustrations* (Biblical Studies Press, 2002).

20. **I'd like for us to close in a conversational prayer, thanking God for all the things we have talked about today. You don't have to, but I'd like it if all of us would participate.**

Worry Less; Live More, Lesson #6
The Practice of Thinking
Good Questions Have Groups Talking
www.joshhunt.com

OPEN:

What is one thing that is on your mind these days?

DIG

1. **Philippians 4.8. What do we learn about Christian living from this verse?**

WHEN I WAS A TEENAGER, my grandmother shared with me a certain Bible verse that grabbed my attention and provoked my interest. Over the years that followed, I kept this verse in front of me and often contemplated its meaning as I experienced my own life unfolding. As I launched my coaching practice in 1991, I began sharing this special verse with clients, curious whether it would touch and challenge them as deeply as it had me.

As time passed, I observed, first with individuals and then with couples and families, that this single passage from the New Testament contained within it the secret to a joy-filled life. By applying this verse to their daily lives, my clients started amplifying the joy they experienced in their marriages, with their parenting, and in their lives as a whole.

Of course, the verse I am referring to is Philippians 4:8:

> Whatever things are true, whatever things are noble, whatever things are just, whatever things are pure, whatever things are lovely, whatever things are of good report, if there is any virtue and if there is anything praiseworthy—meditate on these things. (NKJV)

Today, we live in a culture inundated with negative headlines that spread images of despair and defeat around the globe in a matter of seconds. Wars continue. Children starve. Tragedy strikes. Corruption abounds. Families break. Scandals erupt. Debt grows. Storms rage.

As a result, we have become far too comfortable accepting the unacceptable and viewing the world, our lives, and ourselves in a defeatist way that directly competes with the passionate, joy-filled, and faith-driven people God desires us to be. — Tommy Newberry, *40 Days to a Joy-Filled Life: Living the 4:8 Principle* (Carol Stream, IL: Tyndale House Publishers, Inc., 2012).

2. Imagine you read this verse three times a day over the next ninety days. Imagine you took 60 seconds to think about things that are true and noble and right and pure. How might life change?

Based on Philippians 4:8, the 4:8 Principle states that whatever you give your attention to expands in your experience. If you dwell on your strengths, your blessings, your goals, and all the people who love you, then you will attract even more blessings, even more love, and even more accomplishments. It's a powerful truth. While trials and tribulations are permanent fixtures of this world, our attitudes toward them can help soothe the wounds and bring about solutions while glorifying our heavenly Father in the process. — Tommy

Newberry, *40 Days to a Joy-Filled Life: Living the 4:8 Principle* (Carol Stream, IL: Tyndale House Publishers, Inc., 2012).

3. **Context. How is this verse related to the command stated earlier: rejoice in the Lord always?**

    A HEALTHY BODY produces energy. Likewise, a healthy mind produces joy. This is not an accident. If you want to experience vibrant health and abundant energy, it is essential that you consume certain foods and drinks and refrain from consuming others. The same is true if you want to lose weight or put more muscle on your frame. You have to say yes to the foods that lead you toward your goal and no to those that lead you away. Very simply, you need to eat this, not that. And while, for the most part, this is now considered common sense, it is not always common practice for those desiring to reshape their physical bodies or increase their energy levels.

    Progress toward joy begins the same way, with a firm decision to cut back on joy-reducing thoughts and increase joy-producing thoughts. In short, you have to change your mental diet. You have to think this, not that. After all, joy is the sum and substance of emotional health. — Tommy Newberry, *40 Days to a Joy-Filled Life: Living the 4:8 Principle* (Carol Stream, IL: Tyndale House Publishers, Inc., 2012).

4. **Think on these things. Why is it important what we direct our thoughts toward?**

    The word finally indicates that Paul has arrived at the climax of his teaching on spiritual stability. The principle that he is about to relate is both the summation of all the others and the key to implementing them. The phrase dwell on these things introduces an important truth: spiritual stability is a result of how a person thinks. The imperative form of logizomai (dwell on) makes it a command; proper thinking is not optional in the Christian life. Logizomai means more than just entertaining thoughts; it means "to evaluate," "to consider," or "to calculate." Believers are to consider the qualities Paul lists in this verse and meditate on their implications. The verb form calls for habitual discipline of the mind to set all thoughts on these spiritual virtues.

The Bible leaves no doubt that people's lives are the product of their thoughts. Proverbs 23:7 declares, "For as he thinks within himself, so he is." The modern counterpart to that proverb is the computer acronym GIGO (Garbage In, Garbage Out). Just as a computer's output is dependent on the information that is input, so people's actions are the result of their thinking. Jesus expressed that truth in Mark 7:20–23: "That which proceeds out of the man, that is what defiles the man. For from within, out of the heart of men, proceed the evil thoughts, fornications, thefts, murders, adulteries, deeds of coveting and wickedness, as well as deceit, sensuality, envy, slander, pride and foolishness. All these evil things proceed from within and defile the man."

Paul's call for biblical thinking is especially relevant in our culture. The focus today is on emotion and pragmatism, and the importance of serious thinking about biblical truth is downplayed. People no longer ask "Is it true?" but "Does it work?" and "How will it make me feel?" Those latter two questions serve as a working definition of truth in our society that rejects the concept of absolute divine truth. Truth is whatever works and produces positive emotions. Sadly, such pragmatism and emotionalism has crept even into theology. The church is often more concerned about whether something will be divisive or offensive than whether it is biblically true.

— John F. MacArthur Jr., *Philippians, MacArthur New Testament Commentary* (Chicago: Moody Press, 2001), 285.

5. **Occasionally, you will hear of someone doing some bone-head thing and they will say, "I feel good about it," or, "I have a peace about it." What does this passage have to say about such decision making?**

Too many people go to church not to think or reason about the truths of Scripture, but to get their weekly spiritual high; to feel that God is still with them. Such people are spiritually unstable because they base their lives on feeling rather than on thinking. Bill Hull writes,

> What scares me is the anti-intellectual, anti-critical-thinking philosophy that has spilled over into the Church. This philosophy tends to romanticize the faith, making the local church into an experience center.... Their concept of "church" is that they are spiritual consumers and that the church's job is to meet their felt needs. (Right Thinking [Colorado Springs, Colo: NavPress, 1985], 66)

John Stott also warned of the danger of Christians living by their feelings: "Indeed, sin has more dangerous effects on our faculty of feeling than on our faculty of thinking, because our opinions are more easily checked and regulated by revealed truth than our experiences" (Your Mind Matters [Downers Grove, Ill: InterVarsity, 1972], 16).

God commands people to think. He said to rebellious Israel, "Come now, and let us reason together" (Isa. 1:18). Jesus chided the unbelieving Pharisees and Sadducees for demanding a miraculous sign from Him. Instead, He challenged them to think and draw inferences from the evidence they had, just as they did to predict the weather (Matt. 16:1–3). In Luke 12:57 He said to the crowds, "And why do you not even on your own initiative judge what is right?" God gave His revelation in a book, the Bible, and expects people to use their minds to understand its truths.

Careful thinking is the distinctive mark of the Christian faith. James Orr expressed that reality clearly:

> If there is a religion in the world which exalts the office of teaching, it is safe to say that it is the religion of Jesus Christ. It has been frequently remarked that in pagan religions the doctrinal element is at a minimum—the chief thing there is the performance of a ritual. But this is precisely where Christianity distinguishes itself from other religions—it does contain doctrine. It comes to men with definite, positive teaching; it claims to be the truth; it bases religion on knowledge, though a knowledge which is only attainable under moral conditions. I do not see how any one can deal fairly with the facts as they lie before us in the Gospels and Epistles, without coming to the conclusion that the New Testament is full of doctrine.... A religion divorced from earnest and lofty thought has always, down the whole history of the Church, tended to become weak, jejune, and unwholesome; while the intellect, deprived of its rights within religion, has sought its satisfaction without, and developed into godless rationalism. (The Christian View of God and the World [New York: Scribner, 1897], 20–21)

John F. MacArthur Jr., *Philippians, MacArthur New Testament Commentary* (Chicago: Moody Press, 2001), 285–286.

6. No one can see my thoughts. What difference does it make what I think about?

Almost everything that happens to you, good or bad, originates witha single thought. Neuroscientists can now demonstrate that every thought sends electrical and chemical signals throughout your brain, ultimately affecting each cell in your body. Thoughts can influence your sleep, your digestion, your pulse, the chemical makeup of your blood, and all other bodily functions. The secret conversations you hold in the privacy of your own mind are shaping your destiny, little by little. With every thought that races through your mind, you are continually reinventing yourself and your future. Research indicates that the average person thinks approximately fifty thousand thoughts per day. This is either good or bad news because every thought moves you either toward your God-given potential or away from it. No thoughts are neutral.

> The outer world of circumstance shapes itself to the inner world of thought, and both pleasant and unpleasant external conditions are factors which make for the ultimate good of the individual. As the reaper of his own harvest, man learns both by suffering and bliss. – James Allen

Whatever you direct your mind to think about will ultimately be revealed for everyone to see. Remind yourself with a smile that "my thoughts are showing." See, you have two options: By your manner of thinking, you can draw out the best in yourself and others, or you can draw out the worst. What you persistently think eventually but inevitably crystallizes into the words you speak and then the things you do. — Tommy Newberry, *The 4:8 Principle: The Secret to a Joy-Filled Life* (Carol Stream, IL: Tyndale House Publishers, Inc., 2010).

7. How are our thoughts and our joy related?

Think about what you want, not what you don't want. Why is this required for joy-filled living? Very simply stated, we tend to bring about what we think about. As King Solomon counseled, "As [a person] thinks in his heart, so is he" (Proverbs 23:7, NKJV).

Building on Solomon's wisdom, James Allen wrote that "the outer world of circumstance shapes itself to the inner world of thought, and both pleasant and unpleasant external conditions are factors which make for the ultimate good of the individual. As the reaper of his own harvest, man learns both by suffering and bliss."[1]

It is my intention that during this forty-day regimen, you will start experiencing more of the bliss that is called joy-filled living. Starting today, release the need to hang on to thoughts that haven't worked well for you.

It is true that we can think this, not that! — Tommy Newberry, *40 Days to a Joy-Filled Life: Living the 4:8 Principle* (Carol Stream, IL: Tyndale House Publishers, Inc., 2012).

8. Is it possible to rejoice in the Lord always without giving careful attention to your thoughts?

Many well-meaning individuals desire to be leaner or more energetic but then continue to indulge in a diet and lifestyle that takes them in the opposite direction. Consequently, they do not reach their goal. Many with the goal of increased joy run into the same predicament: they keep consuming a mental diet mismatched with their goal. In both instances, there is a major disconnect between desired objectives and daily behavior.

Joy is a state of mind that must be purposely cultivated if you are to live and love and influence others as God intended. Fortunately, joy does not depend on the outer conditions of your material life, but rather on the inner condition of your mental life. Joy is the result of something strikingly simple, though not necessarily easy: consistently thinking joy-producing thoughts.

Is this within your grasp? Is it even possible for anyone to accomplish? Before you answer, let me remind you that few endeavors worth pursuing come easily to anyone, and the attainment of a joy-filled spirit is no exception. There are risks in shooting for this gold standard of faith in action. There is a high price to be paid, and it must be paid in advance. Certain comfort thoughts will need to be relinquished. Counterproductive habits will need to be abandoned. Tenured excuses must be surrendered. — Tommy Newberry, *40 Days to a Joy-Filled Life: Living the 4:8 Principle* (Carol Stream, IL: Tyndale House Publishers, Inc., 2012).

9. How are my thoughts and my worry related?

Controlling your thoughts is one of the most difficult things to do. You probably find it easy to worry, to daydream, to let your imagination run wild, and to let unbidden thoughts creep in and take over. But, oh, the repercussions of this lack of control.

God tells you in Philippians 4:8 where to direct your thoughts: "Finally, brothers, whatever is true, whatever is noble, whatever is right, whatever is pure, whatever is lovely, whatever is admirable—if anything is excellent or praiseworthy—think about such things."

Daily prayer and Bible study will help you keep your mind on Christ Jesus and will help you stay in God's will. — Bill Dunn and Kathy Leonard, *Through a Season of*

Grief: Devotions for Your Journey from Mourning to Joy (Nashville: Thomas Nelson, 2004).

10. Philippians 4:7 (NIV) "And the peace of God, which transcends all understanding, will guard your hearts and your minds in Christ Jesus." How are our thoughts and our peace of mind related?

Our thoughts play a great role in the level of peace in our lives. When our minds are occupied with negative, nagging, and unproductive thoughts, we push peace away and invite anxiety and worry into our lives. Therefore, we must learn to recognize and replace negative thought patterns before they rob us of peace.

There are seven categories of thoughts that steal peace from us: sinful, negative, erroneous, unrealistic, rebellious, obsessive, and enslaved thoughts. Each category represents a different area in which Satan aims to establish a stronghold in our minds.

Whether you are plagued by one or several of these types of thoughts, it is important to properly extinguish the flames of their fiery path through your mind. Until they are put down, you will be unable to experience God's gift of peace.

When these thoughts surface, first reach out to God in prayer. Confess that you are struggling with troublesome thoughts and ask Him to remove your burden. Then turn your mind's energy to that which is positive, uplifting, and of God.

Philippians 4:8 encourages us to think on things that are true, noble, right, pure, lovely, admirable, excellent, and praiseworthy. Allow God to quench your desire to ponder more negative concepts and ideas with positive thoughts of His plan for peace in your life. — Charles

F. Stanley, *Pathways to His Presence* (Nashville, TN: Thomas Nelson Publishers, 2006), 242.

11. Note the word "whatever." Is this talking about thinking about spiritual things, or would thinking about secular things that are true and right and lovely, etc. count?

The striking word in that command is whatever. Our minds are being shaped all the time, but we have great freedom to pursue minds that flourish. As a bee that can find nectar in all kinds of flowers, we are now free — even commanded — to feed our minds on noble thoughts wherever we find them. The Bible itself commands us to look beyond just the Bible to feed our minds.

Let us meditate for a moment on that phrase "whatever is lovely." Think of something that is "lovely" to you. A sunset. A favorite novel. Tiny robins chirping in the nest. The face of someone you love. Music that makes you dance. Let your mind dwell there for a moment. Give it directed mental focus.

You just obeyed the Bible. That "counts." You just opened up your mind a bit to the flow of the Holy Spirit. — John Ortberg, *The Me I Want to Be* (Grand Rapids, MI: Zondervan, 2009).

12. Look at the list in Philippians 4.8. Is Paul advocating wishful thinking?

There are the things which are true. Many things in this world are deceptive and illusory, promising what they can never perform, offering a false peace and happiness which they can never supply. We should always set our thoughts on the things which will not let us down. — William Barclay, *The Letters to Philippians, Colossians,*

and Thessalonians, 3rd ed. fully rev. and updated.,
The New Daily Study Bible (Louisville, KY; London:
Westminster John Knox Press, 2003), 92.

13. The NIV has the second quality as noble. How does your translation have it?

There are the things which are, as the Authorized
Version has it, honest. This is an archaic use of honest
in the sense of honourable, as the Revised Standard
Version translates it. The Authorized Version suggests
in the margin venerable. The Revised Version has
honourable and suggests in the margin reverent. Moffatt
has worthy.

It can be seen from all this that the Greek (semnos)
is difficult to translate. It is the word which is
characteristically used of the gods and of the temples
of the gods. When used to describe an individual, it
describes a person who, as it has been said, moves
through life as if the whole world were the temple of
God. The nineteenth-century poet and critic Matthew
Arnold suggested the translation nobly serious. But
the word really describes that which has the dignity of
holiness upon it. There are things in this world which
are flippant and cheap and attractive to those who
never take life seriously; but it is on the things which are
serious and dignified that Christians will set their minds.
— William Barclay, *The Letters to Philippians, Colossians,
and Thessalonians, 3rd ed. fully rev. and updated.,
The New Daily Study Bible* (Louisville, KY; London:
Westminster John Knox Press, 2003), 93.

14. Next, we have right (NIV), or just (KJV). What are some examples?

There are the things which are just. The word is dikaios,
and the Greeks defined the person who is dikaios as the

one who gives to gods and to other people what is their due. In other words, dikaios is the word of duty faced and duty done. There are those who set their minds on pleasure, comfort and easy ways. The Christian's thoughts are on duty to other people and duty to God. — William Barclay, *The Letters to Philippians, Colossians, and Thessalonians, 3rd ed. fully rev. and updated., The New Daily Study Bible* (Louisville, KY; London: Westminster John Knox Press, 2003), 93.

15. Pure. To clarify our understanding of this one, let's think about the opposite. What are some examples of things that are impure?

There are the things which are pure. The word is hagnos and describes what is morally uncontaminated. When it is used ceremonially, it describes that which has been so cleansed that it is fit to be brought into the presence of God and used in his service. This world is full of things which are sordid and shabby and soiled and smutty. Many people develop a way of thinking that soils everything. The Christian's mind is set on the things which are pure; the Christian's thoughts are so clean that they can stand even the scrutiny of God. — William Barclay, *The Letters to Philippians, Colossians, and Thessalonians, 3rd ed. fully rev. and updated., The New Daily Study Bible* (Louisville, KY; London: Westminster John Knox Press, 2003), 93–94.

16. Next, lovely. You might see how your translation has it. What is this talking about?

There are the things which the Authorized Version and the Revised Standard Version call lovely. James Moffatt's translation has attractive. The word we have chosen, winsome, a word not so often used today, is the best translation of all. The Greek is prosphilēs, and it might be paraphrased as that which calls forth love.

There are those whose minds are so set on vengeance and punishment that they cause bitterness and fear in others. There are those whose minds are so set on criticism and rebuke that they bring out resentment in others. Christians set their minds on the lovely things—kindness, sympathy, patience—so they are winsome people, whose presence inspires feelings of love. — William Barclay, *The Letters to Philippians, Colossians, and Thessalonians, 3rd ed. fully rev. and updated., The New Daily Study Bible* (Louisville, KY; London: Westminster John Knox Press, 2003), 94.

17. Admirable. The KJV has "of a good report." How does your translation have it? What is this telling us to think about?

There are the things which are, as the Authorized Version has it, of good report. In the margin, the Revised Version suggests gracious. Moffatt has high-toned. The Revised Standard Version has gracious. Charles Kingsley Williams has whatever has a good name. It is not easy to get at the meaning of this word (eophema). It literally means fair-speaking; but it was especially connected with the holy silence at the beginning of a sacrifice in the presence of the gods. It might not be going too far to say that it describes the things which are fit for God to hear. There are far too many ugly words and false words and impure words in this world. On the lips and in the minds of Christians, there should be only words which are fit for God to hear. — William Barclay, *The Letters to Philippians, Colossians, and Thessalonians, 3rd ed. fully rev. and updated., The New Daily Study Bible* (Louisville, KY; London: Westminster John Knox Press, 2003), 94.

18. Finally, think about things that are excellent and praiseworthy. What are some examples?

Paul goes on: if there be any virtue. Both Moffatt and the Revised Standard Version use excellence instead of virtue. The word is aretē. The odd fact is that, although aretē was one of the great classical words, Paul usually seems deliberately to avoid it, and this is the only time it occurs in his writings. In classical thought, it described every kind of excellence. It could describe the excellence of the ground in a field, the excellence of a tool for its purpose, the physical excellence of an animal, the excellence of the courage of a soldier, and the virtue of an individual. Lightfoot suggests that with this word Paul calls in as an ally all that was excellent in the non-Christian background of his friends. It is as if he were saying: 'If the idea of excellence held by the religions in which you were brought up has any influence over you— think of that. Think of your past life at its very highest, to spur you on to the new heights of the Christian way.' The world has its impurities and its degradations, but it also has its fine qualities and its brave actions, and it is of the high things that Christians must think.

Finally, Paul says: if there be any praise. In one sense, it is true that Christians never think of the praise of others, but in another sense it is true that every good individual is uplifted by the praise of good men and women. So Paul says that Christians will live in such a way that they will neither conceitedly desire nor foolishly despise the praise of others. — William Barclay, *The Letters to Philippians, Colossians, and Thessalonians, 3rd ed. fully rev. and updated., The New Daily Study Bible* (Louisville, KY; London: Westminster John Knox Press, 2003), 94–95.

19. How could you apply the Philippians 4.8 principle to your life this week? How could you focus your thoughts on Philippians 4.8 things?

What causes your mind to be drawn to what is true, noble, right, pure, lovely, admirable, excellent, and praiseworthy? Maybe it is taking art classes and learning to see beauty you had never noticed before. One man I know spends much of his time in his car, listening to a list of the twenty best works of English fiction. Maybe you are an athlete, and competition stirs you to admire the pursuit of excellence. What causes your mind to be drawn to those things?

God's desire is for you to have a mind that habitually thinks noble, true, pure, admirable thoughts. You have great freedom — whatever — to allow the Spirit to rewire your mind. As that happens, the Holy Spirit's goal is not to get you really good at suppressing angry behavior. It is for you to have a mind characterized by an ever-increasing flow of Spirit-guided, truth-based, life-producing thoughts and feelings.

When we read about what is noble, when we see something praiseworthy, we experience what psychologist Jonathan Haidt called "elevation." We actually feel a slight expansion in our chest; we feel lighter in our bodies. Our emotions are inspired, and we want to become more excellent ourselves. That counts as obedience to Scripture. That is spiritual.

The flow of the Holy Spirit is always available. You do not have to wait for anything. — John Ortberg, *The Me I Want to Be* (Grand Rapids, MI: Zondervan, 2009).

20. How can we pray for each other this week?

OPEN:

Who most influenced you to come to faith in Christ?

DIG

1. **Philippians 4.9. Who has influenced you in your discipleship? Who has said to you, "Whatever you have learned or received or heard from me, or seen in me—put it into practice"?**

   Discipleship today must also begin with a commitment of submission to at least one other person. Choosing the life begins right here. Without this relational dimension, everything that follows is weakened.

   The teacher-disciple relationship was a powerful bond in the first century. It was as important as and in many cases more crucial than a father-son relationship. It was similar to a servant-master relationship (Matt. 10:24). Once accepted as a disciple, a young man would work his way up the discipleship ladder. He would begin as a talmidh, or beginner, who would be required to sit in the back of the room and not speak. Later he became a distinguished student who could begin taking an independent line in his approach or questioning. The next level was a disciple-associate; at this stage he could sit immediately behind the rabbi during prayer time. The highest level was when the disciple reached "disciple of the wise" status, when he was recognized as the intellectual equal of his rabbi. — Bill Hull, *Choose the Life: Exploring a Faith That Embraces Discipleship* (Grand Rapids, MI: Baker Books, 2004), 32.

2. How confident would you be to say to a new believer, "Whatever you see in me, put it into practice"?

Jesus said, "A disciple … [who] is fully taught will be like his teacher" (Luke 6:40 RSV). The highest calling of any disciple was to imitate his teacher. Paul called upon Timothy to follow his example (2 Tim. 3:10–14), and he didn't hesitate to call upon all believers to do the same (1 Cor. 4:14–16; 11:1; Phil. 4:9; 2 Tim. 2:2). The problem today is that while a pastor may be a good example with regard to character, the pastor usually is not close enough to members of his or her congregation to influence them personally. The pastor's life is distant, insulated from the marketplace and the public square; thus he or she isn't a mentor to the ordinary person.

Finally, in the first century there was a clear, nonnegotiable expectation that every disciple would reproduce in finding and training his own apprentices. He was to start his own school, and he could call it after his name. It was common for a disciple's school to be called the "House of Hillel" or the "House of Joshua." — Bill Hull, *Choose the Life: Exploring a Faith That Embraces Discipleship* (Grand Rapids, MI: Baker Books, 2004), 33.

3. This sounds a little foreign to us. How do you imagine it sounded to the original audience?

The rabbinical model from first-century Israel has something to offer the modern church. The tradition was for a young man to choose a rabbi. (I suppose we would call it "apply to a rabbi.") If accepted, the apprentice would learn from the rabbi about his way of life. He would learn the words of the rabbi, his way of ministry, his life, and his character. In the case of Jesus and his disciples, then: (1) a disciple would choose to follow Jesus; (2) a disciple would learn Jesus' words; (3) a disciple would learn Jesus' way of ministry; (4) a disciple would imitate Jesus' life and character; and (5) a disciple would find and teach other disciples for Jesus.

The disciple-making church might not be as formal, but there is a need for effective pairings where mutual submission would cause disciples to walk together in life. I believe that every adult follower of Jesus must be in submission to Christ through at least one other person besides their spouse. That person is there to teach the apprentice what it means to be a Christ-follower—to believe, live, love, minister, and lead as Jesus himself did. As Paul told his readers, "Keep putting into practice all you learned and received from me—everything you heard from me and saw me doing" (Phil. 4:9 NLT).

The two most obvious areas of need are in the decision to submit ourselves to another person, and then in taking the responsibility to engage others in the same process once we are ready. If we were to ask for a show of hands in a church service of those who are in an apprenticeship relationship, it would be less than 10 percent of the congregation. This again is the great omission in the Great Commission—the lack of apprenticeship, of teaching disciples to obey and do the things Jesus taught us.

There is not a shortage of preaching about Christ or a lack of mission emphasis; they are present in abundance in American churches. The startling lack is in this most fundamental of tasks, the being and making of disciples. Its cure is apprenticeship with relational accountability. It has transformed the church in the past, and it can do so again. — Bill Hull, *The Disciple-Making Church: Leading a Body of Believers on the Journey of Faith, Updated Edition.* (Grand Rapids, MI: Baker Books, 2010), 228.

4. **This one might take a little imagination—or guessing. How do you think our disciplemaking process compares with how they made disciple in the first century?**

The characteristics above describe the institution of discipleship as it was practiced in the first century.14 Jesus implemented this same institution with his closest followers, and they were expected to reproduce. When he called upon them to make disciples, they were to find others who would make the commitments above. When he told them to "[teach] them to obey everything I have commanded you" (Matt. 28:20), they knew it would require the kind of dedication outlined above.

There was a crucial difference, however, in Jesus' teaching, which is shown in his strong reaction to the Pharisees' hypocrisy. He scolded them for their selfish ambition and propensity for showmanship.

> They love to be greeted in the marketplaces and to have men call them "Rabbi." But you are not to be called "Rabbi," for you have only one Master and you are all brothers. And do not call anyone on earth "father," for you have one Father, and he is in

heaven. Nor are you to be called "teacher," for you have one Teacher, the Christ. The greatest among you will be your servant. For whoever exalts himself will be humbled, and whoever humbles himself will be exalted. Matthew 23:7–12

The New Testament does refer to people as teachers, elders, and so on, but that was not Jesus' meaning in this passage. He was speaking against being a slave or servant to any master other than himself. As a disciple in the first century, you followed your master and did whatever he told you to do. If you ever asked your rabbi a question, you were bound by his answer. That is why people were cautious about asking their teacher questions.

The distinction that Jesus made was that his disciples were not to raise up new disciples for themselves. They were not to start their own school or academy. The disciples of Jesus were never to take the role of master. In fact, Jesus' disciples were forbidden to make their own disciples. They were to raise up more disciples for Jesus, and the same is true today. Yes, we will have teachers, mentors, and leaders, but they never will become our masters. The job of Jesus' disciples today is the same as it was in the first century. We are called to follow Jesus and to raise up more disciples for him.
— Bill Hull, *Choose the Life: Exploring a Faith That Embraces Discipleship* (Grand Rapids, MI: Baker Books, 2004), 33–34.

5. How did Jesus go about making disciples? What was his method?

It all started by Jesus calling a few men to follow him. This revealed immediately the direction his evangelistic strategy would take. His concern was not with programs to reach the multitudes, but with men whom the multitudes would follow. Remarkable as it may seem, Jesus started to gather these men before he ever organized an evangelistic campaign or even preached a sermon in public. Men were to be his method of winning the world to God. — Robert E. Coleman, *The Master Plan of Evangelism* (Grand Rapids, MI: Revell, 2006), 21.

6. Would you say Jesus' method was formal or informal?

Having called his men, Jesus made a practice of being with them. This was the essence of his training program—just letting his disciples follow him.

When one stops to think of it, this was an incredibly simple way of doing it. Jesus had no formal school, no seminaries, no outlined course of study, no periodic membership classes in which he enrolled his followers. None of these highly organized procedures considered so necessary today entered into his ministry. Amazing as it may seem, all Jesus did to teach these men his way was to draw them close to himself. He was his own school and curriculum.

The natural informality of this teaching method of Jesus stood in striking contrast to the formal, almost scholastic procedures of the scribes. These religious teachers insisted on their disciples adhering strictly to certain rituals and formulas of knowledge which distinguished them from others; whereas Jesus asked only that his disciples follow him. Knowledge was not communicated by the Master in terms of laws and dogmas, but in the living personality of One who walked among them. His disciples were distinguished, not by outward conformity to certain rituals, but by being with him, and thereby participating in his doctrine (John 18:19). — Robert E. Coleman, *The Master Plan of Evangelism* (Grand Rapids, MI: Revell, 2006), 33–34.

7. **Would you say that Jesus concentrated on the many or the few? Why do you think He did what He did?**

Here is the wisdom of his method, and in observing it, we return again to the fundamental principle of concentration on those he intended to use. One cannot transform a world except as individuals in the world are transformed, and individuals cannot be changed except as they are molded in the hands of the Master. The necessity is apparent not only to select a few helpers but also to keep the group small enough to be able to work effectively with them.

Hence, as the company of followers around Jesus increased, it became necessary by the middle of his second year of ministry to narrow the select company to a more manageable number. Accordingly Jesus "called his disciples, and he chose from them twelve, whom also he named apostles" (Luke 6:13–17; see Mark 3:13–19). Regardless of the symbolical meaning one prefers to put on the number twelve,3 it is clear that Jesus intended these men to have unique privileges and responsibilities in the Kingdom work.

This does not mean that Jesus' decision to have twelve apostles excluded others from following him, for as we know, many more were numbered among his associates, and some of these became very effective workers in the church. The seventy (Luke 10:1); Mark, the Gospel writer; and James, his own brother (1 Cor. 15:7; Gal. 2:9, 12; see John 2:12; 7:2–10), are notable examples of this. Nevertheless, we must acknowledge that there was a rapidly diminishing priority given to those outside the Twelve. — Robert E. Coleman, *The Master Plan of Evangelism* (Grand Rapids, MI: Revell, 2006), 23–24.

8. **Philippians 4.9 teaches the importance of an example. Can you think of—or find—other**

verses that speak to the importance of setting an example?

Example gives credibility to leadership. People are far more impressed by what they see than what they hear. Paul reminded the elders of Ephesus how he had kept back nothing that was for their good and had "showed" them all things (20:20, 35). Writing to the church at Philippi, he said: "The things which ye both learned and received and heard and saw in me, these things do ..." (Phil. 4:9). He did not invite disciples to follow a theory, but a person. That person was Jesus Christ, the only Lord and Savior. But they were to follow Christ as Paul followed Him (1 Cor. 11:1). The apostle's life was not the end of their quest, but it was an example of one seeking with all his heart and soul to be a disciple of Christ (Phil. 3:17; 1 Thess. 2:8; 2 Tim. 1:13; cf. John 13:15). — Robert Emerson Coleman, *The Master Plan of Discipleship* (Old Tappan, NJ: Fleming H. Revell Company, 1987), 85.

9. **Imagine our pastor called and asked you to disciple a new convert. What would you do?**

A Life Transformation Group is made up of two to three people, all of the same gender, who meet weekly for personal accountability in the areas of their spiritual growth and development. A group should not grow beyond three but multiply into two groups of two rather than a single group of four. If a fourth person is added to the group, it is recommended that the group consider itself "pregnant" and ready to give birth to a second group. After the fourth person has demonstrated sufficient faithfulness to the group for two to three weeks, the group should multiply into two groups of two.

There is no curriculum or training needed for the LTG. A simple bookmark that stays in the participant's Bible is all that is needed. The LTG accountability consists of three essential disciplines for personal spiritual growth—a steady diet of Scripture, confession of sin, and prayer for others who need Christ...

https://www.cmaresources.org/article/ltg

10. We have been talking about making disciples. Perhaps we should back up. What is a disciple?

A disciple is one who is being changed by Jesus. He is making us into someone different. He changes hearts, which means our attitudes and priorities begin to shift. This kind of change is supernatural and is evidenced by a love for God and for others. The Holy Spirit is making us into relational people with an eternal perspective. God intends to use these relationships to lead a broken world to the transforming power of Jesus. His power makes these relationships possible. — Jim Putman et al., *Real-Life Discipleship Training Manual: Equipping Disciples Who Make Disciples* (Colorado Springs, CO: NavPress, 2010), 33.

11. John 8.31. What is the difference between a disciple and a convert?

Leroy Eims, who teaches that the goal of the Christian's life—especially the new Christian—is someday to become a disciple, writes: "The commission of Christ to you was to make disciples, not just get converts. So your objective now is to help this new Christian progress to the point where he is a fruitful, mature, and dedicated disciple."5 Thus a disciple is a mature, fruitful, dedicated believer. He also writes that typically it takes approximately two years for a new convert to become a disciple.6

This model implies that there are basically two kinds or classes of Christians in the church. The first are ordinary believers, and the second are committed believers who are following Christ as his disciples. And all of us who are believers fall into one category or the other. — Aubrey Malphurs, *Strategic Disciple Making: A Practical Tool for Successful Ministry* (Grand Rapids, MI: Baker, 2009), 29–30.

12. Jesus said, "If you hold to my teaching you are really my disciples." What does it mean to hold to Jesus teaching?

A transaction with Jesus in the past that has no ongoing expression in our lives was a false transaction. When Jesus said, "If you abide in my word, you are truly my disciples" (John 8:31), he meant that if we don't abide, we are not truly his disciples. And the opposite of true disciples is false disciples. That's what we are if we count on past experiences without ongoing devotion to Jesus. — John Piper, *What Jesus Demands from the World* (Wheaton, IL: Crossway Books, 2006), 62.

13. Psalm 138.8. Look this up in several translations. What do we learn about God from this verse?

The LORD will fulfill his purpose for me; your steadfast love, O LORD, endures forever. Do not forsake the work of your hands. (Psalm 138:8)

My friend David Powlison says that it is the King of the universe who leads us into fiery trials with the purpose of meeting us there. His leading is not without love and purpose. God is Father as well as King. In all that he does, he always acts with gracious and loving purposefulness. That includes suffering. He leads us into suffering, even through the valley of the shadow of death, for his purpose in our lives—a kind, gracious, and high purpose. God, the Father, meets us in our suffering. God, the Son, comes alongside us as fellow sufferer, One who has faced death and defeated it. God, the Spirit, fills us with the power that raised Jesus from the dead and reminds us of the glorious inheritance we have in Christ. God addresses our hearts and draws us to himself.

Psalm 138:8 has been a great encouragement about God's grace in my life (and every life). He will fulfill his purpose for me precisely because his faithful love endures forever. — Elizabeth W. D. Groves, *Grief Undone: A Journey with God and Cancer* (Greensboro, NC: New Growth Press, 2015).

14. How does the Lord fulfill his purpose in us?

Whenever I speak on the subject of every one of us being here on earth for a reason, these questions inevitably come up: "But what about people with disabilities? Does God have a purpose for them? Or did He make a mistake when He made them?"

Let me tell you about Dr. John and Christine Haggai's son, Johnny, who was born with severe cerebral palsy. He could not talk or walk or feed himself and required care twenty-fours a day. He lived to be only twenty-four years old.

An intoxicated doctor's negligence caused Johnny to be born with these acute limitations. But his parents chose to accept his birth as God's divine design for them. They devoted countless hours to his care, seeing him as an incredible blessing. Dr. Haggai said,

Chris and I are thoroughly convinced that Johnny came to us in the sovereign and loving will of God. Johnny lived a significant life. Significant not just because there is worth in every person, as there surely is, but. . . [Johnny] had a role to fill, a destiny to realize.1

Rather than being a burden, Johnny enhanced his parents' lives and inspired them to push on in Christian ministry.

Our culture strongly values perfection—the beautiful woman, the athletic man, the skillful artist, or gifted musician. Yet clearly the Bible points to a purpose for each of us being here—even if we are what the world sees as "broken." Encouraging is Psalm 138:8 that says, "The LORD will perfect that which concerneth me." Let Him use you—whatever your limitations—to bless someone today. — Darlene Sala, *You Are Chosen: Inspiration to Reassure Your Soul* (Uhrichsville, OH: Barbour Publishing, Inc., 2014).

15. Philippians 4.9. One of the way Paul passed on truth to the Philippians was through live teaching and preaching. Another way was through writing. This reminds us that one way we can be discipled is through the writing of others. What books have influenced your walk with God?

Off the top of my head, here are some of my favorites:

- J.I. Packer, *Knowing God*

- R.C. Sproul, *The Holiness of God*

- John Piper, *Desiring God*

- Henry Blackaby, *Experiencing God*

- C.S. Lewis, Mere Christianity

- C.S. Lewis, Screwtape Letters

- C.S. Lewis, The Great Divorce

16. Imagine a young Christian was fired up and asked you to recommend some good Christian books. What books come to mind?

While the most important book any Christian should be reading is the Bible, it's beneficial for us to read books in addition to it. We grow in our faith not only through the Holy Spirit's work in revealing the Scriptures to us, but God also uses the encouragement and gifts of other believers to do so.

Most of us get this, but when it comes to actually getting down to brass tacks and picking books, we're not so sure where to start. At least, this was my experience as a brand-new Christian. When I came to faith, I wound up reading a whole pile of garbage very early on. I really needed was some guidance from another believer, a little help being pointed in the right direction.

And although I can't go back in time and give this guidance to myself, I can pass it along to new believers today. So, here are five books I think every new Christian should read:

Essential Truths of the Christian Faith by R.C. Sproul. There are a lot of really great books on the key teachings of the faith, but this is my top-choice for an entry level introduction to Christian theology. It's greatest strength? Each doctrine is explained in bit-sized chunks using plain language.

Lit! A Christian Guide to Reading Books by Tony Reinke. One of the big challenges new believers have is relearning to read. Specifically, how do you read Christianly. And contrary to popular opinion, this doesn't mean turning our brains off—it means reading even more intently than you may have in the past. (For more on this book, check out my review.)

Just Do Something by Kevin DeYoung. In what I hope will be the last recent(ish) release on this list, Kevin DeYoung's book answers a big, important question: how do I know God's will for my life? This is a question that came to the forefront very early on for me, and the answers provided were (and are) astoundingly helpful. (And if you're interested, here [and here] are a few more thoughts on this book.)

A Call to Prayer by J.C. Ryle. Prayer is a strange and awkward thing for new believers (actually, it's strange and awkward for a lot of us who aren't so new in the faith, too), but it's one of the most essential things we can do as Christians. This little book offers great encouragement in pursuing prayer with vigor.

Morning and Evening by Charles Spurgeon. Not every book needs to be about teaching you how to do something in the Christian life—sometimes you just need some great encouragement. These daily readings from Charles Spurgeon have encouraged Christians for more than 100 years, and I've no doubt they'll continue to for many years to come. https://www.

bloggingtheologically.com/2014/05/14/5-books-every-new-christian-should-read/

17. Paul said, the things you have heard... It reminds of the importance of hearing the Word. This is easier than it has ever been. Assuming you have a smart phone, it is so easy to sign up for a podcast of your favorite preacher. Who are some of your favorites?

John Ortberg, Andy Stanley, David Jeremiah, Rick Warren.

18. Morgan closes this chapter with the story of Henrietta Mears—and ordinary woman whose influence has made a huge difference in a whole generation of people. Who can recall her story?

If you pastor a large church, you might be tempted to overcomplicate the task and may then shrink from attempting it. It is good to remember Henrietta Mears—"Teacher" in the eyes of everyone who knew her. Miss Mears's primary job was Christian Education Director at Hollywood Presbyterian Church in the mid-twentieth century. She also taught a Sunday School class numbering hundreds of university students. But her great legacy grows from her practice of cooking breakfast for a group of no more than eight young men each Saturday morning. Over the decades faces changed while the basic theme remained steady: "My job as a trainer of leaders is to spot the potential of a person.... It doesn't matter if he is doing anything now or not. I must see where he is capable of going. Then I encourage him along that line."[1]

Miss Mears's disciples included Bill Bright, who multiplied her model into a little organization called Campus Crusade for Christ. Other disciples launched Gospel Light Press, Forest Home Christian Conference

Center, Young Life and a host of other Christian organizations. The essential element here is a committed teacher instilling vision and tools in a handful of ordinary people—pretty much the same thing Jesus did for those three-and-a-half years with His disciples.

Back in 1944, the "D" in D-Day simply stood for "day." It was a way of keeping the actual date secret, as was "H-Hour." For our purposes, you might think of D-Day as the day you decide to do something about the thoughts that are running around in your brain at this moment.

You can do this. The assignment has little to do with money, size or talent. You could launch a movement by meeting informally with a group of young leaders. — Ralph Moore and Ed Stetzer, *How to Multiply Your Church: The Most Effective Way to Grow* (Grand Rapids, MI: Baker, 2009).

19. What do you want to remember and apply from today's study?

20. How can we pray for each other this week?

OPEN:

Complete this sentence… my idea of a peaceful day is…

DIG

1. **Philippians 4.4 – 9. What do we learn about God from this passage?**

   The apostle Paul often referred to the Lord as the God of peace. In Romans he said, "Now the God of peace be with you all" (15:33). In 2 Corinthians he wrote, "The God of love and peace will be with you"(13:11). And to the Thessalonian believers he said, may the Lord of peace Himself give you peace always in every way" (2 Thess. 3:16).

   Today's verse emphasizes the fact that God's character is peace. He is the origin and giver of peace. When we have godly attitudes, thoughts, and actions, the peace of God and the God of peace will guard us. His peace provides comfort, tranquility, quietness, and confidence in the midst of any trial you may face. — John MacArthur, *Truth for Today : A Daily Touch of God's Grace* (Nashville, Tenn.: J. Countryman, 2001), 359.

2. **And the God of peace will be with you. This word peace is a big deal in Scripture. It is much more than our concept of peace. What do you know about the Biblical concept of peace?**

Who hasn't longed for peace, living in a world that is so often full of strife? The Hebrew word for peace, however, means much more than the absence of conflict or the end of turmoil. Shalom conveys not only a sense of tranquility but also of wholeness and completion. To enjoy shalom is to enjoy health, satisfaction, success, safety, well-being, and prosperity. Though the New Testament does not directly call Jesus the Prince of Peace, this title from Isaiah has traditionally been associated with him as the one who brings peace to the world. Furthermore, Paul assured the Ephesian Christians saying of Jesus, "He himself is our peace" (Ephesians 2:14). When you pray to Sar Shalom, you are praying to Christ himself. To live in peace is to live in his presence. — Ann Spangler, *The Names of God* (Grand Rapids, MI: Zondervan, 2011).

3. **The Old Testament word is Shalom. What do you know about this rich word?**

This world can be a better place. God wants everyday people like you and me to make this world just a bit more like heaven.

In one small corner of His grand creation, God created a place that was a lot like heaven. He named it Eden. The Garden State was not just beautiful, it was perfect—a piece of heaven on earth. Pain was absent, poverty was unheard of, food was everywhere, and disease was nowhere ... and best of all, everybody (well, all two of them) walked close to God.

However, being the humans we are, things went sideways. We tried to deceive God. This one act, this one moment changed everything. This wrongness called sin began to spread and multiply and reproduce like a mutating virus.1

But here's the good news in all of this—life can still be beautiful. God is still present, and He's doing good today through people who love Him and want to love others in the same way His Son loved you and me.

We all have this feeling deep in our souls that life can be different, that life can be so much more beautiful than it is. Families are not supposed to be broken. Children are not supposed to be abandoned when their mothers die from AIDS. Fathers are not supposed to lose their jobs. Women are not supposed to be held back because of their gender. And people should never experience prejudice because of their race.

God has a more beautiful way.

John Ortberg, in his deeply insightful way, explains the rich meaning behind the ancient Hebrew word shalom.2 The Old Testament prophets spoke about a coming day when God would change the way things are and make this world beautiful again; to describe this, the Jews used the word shalom.3 The word literally means "to be perfect or complete." When the Jews dream about peace they use the word shalom. When King David wrote about peace, he used the word shalom. The word can mean safe. Or maybe this says it best—when life is just right. — Palmer Chinchen, *True Religion: Taking Pieces of Heaven to Places of Hell on Earth* (Colorado Springs, CO: David C. Cook, 2010).

4. **Let's look at this phrase, "the God of peace." This same phrase is used in Romans 16.20. What do we learn about God from this verse?**

For those who turn away from false teachers and who are wise in what is good and innocent in what is evil, the God of peace will soon crush Satan under their feet. Paul assures faithful believers that they can look forward to the day when their spiritual warfare will be over. Teachers of deceit and falsehood are instruments of the devil, and they will be destroyed when the God of peace crushes Satan. In Romans 15:33, Paul refers to "the God of peace" in relation to His divine provision for His children. Here the God of peace is spoken of in relation to His permanent victory over Satan and his minions on behalf of His children. Paul uses the figure of Genesis 3:15, where, after the Fall, God declares to the serpent (Satan) that "He [the Messiah] shall bruise you on the head," that is, inflict a mortal wound. — John F. MacArthur Jr., *Romans, vol. 2, MacArthur New Testament Commentary* (Chicago: Moody Press, 1991), 377.

5. **What do we learn about the devil?**

Since Satan fell, he's been super-busy. His major goal? To build his kingdom. In order for his kingdom to grow, he needs to include as many people as possible. That means you and I are prime candidates for what, on the surface, appear to be very attractive, top-notch positions. What "apple" is he dangling in front of your nose right now? Beware of the lures Satan uses—in a short time apples rot.

Father, help me to be aware of the way in which Satan strikes for my weakest spot, my "Achilles heel." Help me to remember that he is too powerful for me to argue with on my own. Help me to turn my back on him and walk away after I have rebuked him in Your name. Thank You for the assurance You have given us that You will crush Satan under Your feet. — Joy Jacobs, *They Were Women Too: Women of the Old Testament in Devotions for Today* (Chicago, IL: Wingspread, 1981).

6. What do we learn about the peace of God?

The passage closes with a most thought-provoking suggestion. Paul says that the God of peace will soon crush and overthrow Satan, the power of evil. We must note that the peace of God is the peace of action and of victory. There is a kind of peace which can be had at the cost of evading all issues and refusing all decisions, a peace which comes from lethargic inactivity. Christians must always remember that the peace of God is not the peace which has submitted to the world, but the peace which has overcome the world. — William Barclay, *The Letter to the Romans, 3rd ed. fully rev. & updated., The New Daily Study Bible* (Louisville, KY; London: Westminster John Knox Press, 2002), 258.

7. Soon. When will this happen?

The phrase en tachei, here translated soon, has the meaning of speedily, or quickly, as it is rendered in Acts 12:7 and 22:18, and often carried the secondary connotation of unexpectedly. The closely related adverb tachu is used three times in Revelation 22 in relation to Christ's "coming quickly" (vv. 7, 12, 20). We know from the New Testament itself that Satan was not soon crushed from the perspective of believers living at that time. He is still not yet subdued.

It is encouraging that the Lord will crush Satan under your feet, the feet of God's people, as they join Christ in His triumph over Satan. — John F. MacArthur Jr.,

Romans, vol. 2, MacArthur New Testament Commentary (Chicago: Moody Press, 1991), 377.

8. 1 Thessalonians 5.23 – 24. What is the God of peace up to in this passage?

God of peace. While the title "God of love and peace" occurs only in 2 Corinthians 13:11, God the Father is titled the "God of peace" five times (Rom. 15:33; 16:20; Phil. 4:9; 1 Thess. 5:23; Heb. 13:20). The New International Encyclopedia of Bible Words notes that "in the Epistles, 'peace' is most often that restored wholeness that Jesus brings to our relationship with God and others, although this cannot be separated from the inner sense of well-being that accompanies them" (p. 481). New Testament verses that use this title suggest several aspects of the peace that God provides. — Larry Richards, *Every Name of God in the Bible, Everything in the Bible Series* (Nashville, TN: Thomas Nelson, 2001), 131.

9. What do we learn about Christian living from this passage?

"The God of peace Himself sanctify you wholly." If we are to be sanctified, it must be by the God of peace Himself. The power that makes the life of the saint does not come from our efforts at all, it comes from the heart of the God of peace. America has a phrase—"Pray through." What we have to "pray through" is all our petulant struggling after sanctification, all the inveterate suspicion in our hearts that God cannot sanctify us. When we are rid of all that and are right before God, then God lets us see how He alone does the work. — Oswald Chambers, *If Ye Shall Ask* (Hants UK: Marshall, Morgan & Scott, 1996).

10. **One more cross-reference. Hebrews 13.20 – 21. What do we learn about the God of peace from this passage?**

It is God working in us that enables us to do anything worthwhile for His kingdom. We obey God, do His will, and please Him only by relying on the Holy Spirit who dwells within us. — Charles F. Stanley, *The Charles F. Stanley Life Principles Bible: New King James Version* (Nashville, TN: Nelson Bibles, 2005), Heb 13:20–21.

11. **What tends to rob you of peace?**

It is easy to get overcommitted, burned out, bummed out, worn out, and stressed out if you are trying to keep up with too many commitments. It is out of balance to try to do everything. If you are happy doing what you do, keep doing it. But if it wears you out and robs you of peace, don't do it. What sense does it make to commit to something, and then murmur and complain about it while you are doing it?

Being overcommitted will frustrate you. Anxiety is usually a sign that God never told you to do what you are doing in the first place. To avoid frustration in your life, keep in balance. — Joyce Meyer, *Starting Your Day Right: Devotions for Each Morning of the Year* (New York City, NY: FaithWords, 2004).

12. **This is our last week in this study. Let's review what we have learned. First, rejoicing. Why is it important—so important to be repeated repeatedly in this letter—and how do we rejoice?**

Jesus said, "I came that they might have life and have it abundantly" (John 10:10). The word translated "abundantly" suggests something profuse or extraordinary in quantity and quality —a surpassingly happy life. Similarly, Scripture describes eternal life not just as life that doesn't end but as full and satisfying: "God gave us eternal life, and this life is in his Son" (1 John 5:11). The phrase "eternal life" appears forty-three times in the New Testament. It means far more than eternal existence —it means eternal happiness!

In Hebrews 3:13, God calls us to happiness this way: "Encourage each other daily, while it is still called today" (HCSB). If God wants us to be happy in him, today (not tomorrow) is the time to experience Christ-centered happiness.

If we believe in the sovereign God who offered us the redemptive grace of Jesus and we aren't happy, we should ask ourselves why.

Choosing to rejoice by rehearsing reasons to be happy and grateful even in the midst of suffering is an affirmation of trust not only in what God has done but also in our belief that he will bring a good end to all that troubles us. The gospel infuses hope and joy into our circumstances because it acknowledges God's greatness over any crisis we'll face. — Randy Alcorn, *Happiness* (Carol Stream, IL: Tyndale House Publishers, Inc., 2015).

13. **"Let your gentleness be evident to all." What does gentleness look like in the real world—in your real world? What does it look like for you to be gentle to your spouse or to be gentle at work?**

In the old days of training horses, some of them were ridden for hours until they gave in to the control of the rider. Gentleness was produced through force. But animals such as oxen were tamed by placing a young untrained animal in a yoke with a mature ox who became an example for the younger one. That is the picture today's Scripture provides of the gentle nature of Jesus. He doesn't ride us like a bronc-buster to produce gentleness in us. Rather He teaches us gentleness by His example. Jesus was gentle, and we are expected to be gentle also. Paul said that our spiritual wardrobe should include a garment of gentleness: "Therefore, as God's chosen people, holy and dearly loved, clothe yourselves with compassion, kindness, humility, gentleness and patience" (Colossians 3:12).

How can gentleness be displayed in your marriage? One of the best ways is through your communication. Be gentle in the choice of your words. Gentle words are comforting, soothing, and encouraging. Be gentle in your tone of voice; its impact is far greater than your actual words. Harshness in your words can grate like coarse sandpaper.

Our conduct is another way in which we can reflect a gentle spirit. Paul said, "If someone is caught in a sin, you who are spiritual should restore him gently" (Galatians 6:1). Spouses sin against one another in many ways. Holding a grudge or putting down your mate is not a reflection of gentleness. Faults should be handled with gentle forgiveness and restoration. Our goal in marriage is to exercise gentleness toward our spouse. May gentleness be reflected in your marriage relationship! — H. Norman Wright, *Quiet Times for Couples* (Eugene, OR: Harvest House, 2011).

14. "The Lord is near." How does this awareness change your Monday morning?

The Lord Jesus Christ encompasses all believers with His presence (Ps. 119:151). When you have a thought, the Lord is near to read it; when you pray, the Lord is near to hear it; when you need His strength and power, He is near to provide it. In fact, He lives in you and is the source of your spiritual life. An awareness of His presence will keep you from being anxious or unstable.

Knowing the Lord is near helps us "be anxious for nothing" because we know He can handle everything we encounter. Fretting and worrying indicate a lack of trust in God. Either you've created another god who can't help you, or else you believe God could help you but refuses, which means you are questioning His integrity and Word. So delight in the Lord and meditate on His Word (Ps. 1:2). Know who He is and how He acts. Then you'll be able to say, "The Lord is near, so I'm not going to worry." — John MacArthur, *Truth for Today: A Daily Touch of God's Grace* (Nashville, Tenn.: J. Countryman, 2001), 343.

15. "Do not be anxious." Or, as the Living has it, "Don't worry about anything." Easier said than done, right? How do you stop worrying when you are tempted to worry?

The worrisome heart pays a high price for doing so. Worry comes from the Greek word that means "to divide the mind." Anxiety splits us right down the middle, creating a double-minded thinker. Rather than take away tomorrow's trouble, worry voids today's strength. Perception is divided, distorting your vision. Strength is divided, wasting your energy. Who can afford to lose power?

But how can we stop doing so? Paul offers a two-pronged answer: God's part and our part. Our part includes prayer and gratitude. "Don't worry about anything; instead, pray about everything. Tell God what you need, and thank him for all he has done" (Phil. 4:6 NLT, emphasis mine).

God's part? "If you do this, you will experience God's peace, which is far more wonderful than the human mind can understand" (Phil. 4:7 NLT). — Max Lucado, *Grace for the Moment® Volume Ii: More Inspirational Thoughts for Each Day of the Year* (Nashville: Thomas Nelson, 2006).

16. "With thanksgiving." Quick. What is one physical thing, and one spiritual thing you are grateful for?

As human beings, we all struggle with selfishness and ingratitude. We can pray and believe God for something, and even be very thankful and grateful for it when we receive it. But it doesn't take us very long until we are no longer thankful and grateful for them, but actually come to think we are entitled to them.

If we aren't careful, we can even develop a demanding attitude in our relationship with the Lord. We can become upset and aggravated when the Lord doesn't give us everything we think we are entitled to. As His children, we do have an inheritance, but a humble attitude is necessary to receive it. A humble attitude pleases God and will keep our hearts grateful for every blessing we receive. — Joyce Meyer, *The Power of Being Thankful: 365 Devotions for Discovering the Strength of Gratitude* (New York City, NY: FaithWords, 2014).

17. Philippians 4.8. What benefits come to those who finally do something to change their stinkin thinkin?

Christ during the storm—is largely dependent on what we feed our minds. This is how we are able to focus on the Savior rather than the storm.

I want to introduce you to two laws that govern your life. The first is what might be called the law of cognition:

You are what you think. Psychologist Archibald Hart writes, "Research has shown that one's thought life influences every aspect of one's being." Whether we are filled with confidence or fear depends on the kind of thoughts that habitually occupy our minds.

Over the last thirty years or so, the most dominant movement in American psychology is what is known as cognitive psychology—built around the truth that the way you think is the single most determinative thing about you:

The way you think creates your attitudes; the way you think shapes your emotions; the way you think governs your behavior; the way you think deeply influences your immune system and vulnerability to illness. Everything about you flows out of the way you think.

I believe this is one of those cases where we are simply coming to confirm what the writers of Scripture knew quite clearly all along. Paul said, "Do not be conformed to this world, but be transformed by the renewing of your minds." — John Ortberg, *If You Want to Walk on Water, You've Got to Get out of the Boat* (Grand Rapids, MI: Zondervan, 2008).

18. Philippians 4.9. What did we learn about Christian living from this verse? What are we to put into practice?

The Philippian believers were instructed to practice the things they had heard, seen, learned, and received from Paul. The items on that action list included:

- Loving more

- Having greater discernment

- Being sincere and without offense

- Being filled with the fruits of righteousness

- Having conduct worthy of the gospel

- Standing fast in one spirit

- Striving together for the gospel

- Being like-minded, of one accord

- Esteeming others better than themselves

- Working out their own salvation in fear and trembling

- Doing all things without complaining and disputing

- Holding fast the Word of Life

When Paul spoke of the things learned and received, he was talking about careful exhortation. When he spoke of those things heard and seen, he was referring to concrete example. Paul was a living example of the conduct he expected from the Philippians. — David Jeremiah, *David Jeremiah Morning and Evening Devotions: Holy Moments in the Presence of God* (Nashville: Thomas Nelson, 2017).

19. We covered lots of territory today. What do you want to remember and apply?

20. How can we pray for each other this week?

28470398R00079

Printed in Great Britain
by Amazon